REflections

Book 3

Ultimate questions and answers

Ina Taylor

Acknowledgements
Folens Publishers would like to thank the following for giving permission to use copyright material.

Scriptures are taken from the *Good News Bible* published by The Bible Societies/Collins © American Bible Society. Quotes from the Qur'an are taken from *The Koran: With parallel Arabic text*, trans. N.J. Dawood, published by Penguin (1995).

Photo Acknowledgements
©2003 Charles Walker/TopFoto.co.uk: 19
©2003 Topham Picturepoint/TopFoto.co.uk: 16 (top)
Antonia Rolls – Jesus on the Tube: 119 (top)
Anup Shah/naturepl.com: 92
Ark Religion/Helene Rogers: 56, 76
Churches Advertising Network: 116
Corbis Sygma/Hekimian Julien: 15, 21
Corbis Sygma/Polak Matthew: 64, 77
Corbis Sygma: Jacques Langeuin: 49 (top)
Corbis/Adrian Arbib: 36
Corbis/Ashley Cooper: 70–71
Corbis/Bettmann: 63
Corbis/Clouds Hill Imaging Ltd: 24
Corbis/Daane Hoff/Beateworks: 45 (bottom)
Corbis/David Turnley: 23, 65
Corbis/Dennis di Ciccol: 45 (top), 85 (bottom)
Corbis/Fabian Cevallos: 78
Corbis/Gabe Palmer: 58
Corbis/Gianni Giansanti: 65, 73 (top), 81
Corbis/Jamie Harron/Papilio: 18 (top)
Corbis/Jehad Nga: 5
Corbis/Joe McDonald: 84
Corbis/John Periam/Cordaiy: 4
Corbis/Lester Lefkowitz: 26
Corbis/London Aerial Photograph Library: 44 (top)
Corbis/Macduff Everton: 44 (bottom), 57
Corbis/Mark Peterson: 42
Corbis/Matthias Rulkafzefal: 28
Corbis/Mediscan: 29
Corbis/Myron Jay Dorf: 98
Corbis/Patrick Ward: 39
Corbis/Peter Schouten/National Geographic Society/Reuters/Corbis: 93
Corbis/Peter Turnley: 17
Corbis/Reuters: 22, 25,33,38 (top), 43
Corbis/Roger Ressmeyer: 86
Corbis/Rune Hellestad: 6
Corbis/Sean Adair/Reuters: 8
Corbis/STScl/NASA: 95
Corbis: 18 (bottom)
Corbis: 46, 58–59, 102
Film: Jesus of Nazareth, AKG-images: 115
Getty: 54
Getty Images Entertainment/Scoopt: 102
Getty Images/AFP: 25, 38 (bottom)
Getty Images/Time & Life Pictures: 68
Getty Images: 16 (bottom), 52, 105 (bottom), 107
Getty/Gioliano Fornari: 62
Getty/Imagno/Austrian Archives: 7
Getty/Lisa Peardon: 11
Getty/Lucas Cranach the Elder: 10
Getty/SMC Images: 94
Getty/Time & Life Pictures: 12
Ina Taylor: 48, 49 (bottom), 61, 73 (bottom), 109, 121
iStockphoto/Anneke Schram: 5
iStockphoto/Brandon Laufenberg: 90
iStockphoto/Darryl Sleath: 66–67
iStockphoto/Jakub Semeniuk: 97 (right)
iStockphoto/Jamaludin Abu Semas: 97 (left)
iStockphoto/Jaroslaw Baczewski: 112
iStockphoto/Juston Long: 5
iStockphoto/Kenneth C. Zirkel: 30
iStockphoto/Matt Trommer: 82
iStockphoto/Pattie Calfy: 113
iStockphoto/Paul Maton: 96
iStockphoto: 79, 101, 103
iStsockphoto/Andrea Laurila: 51
John Reilly The Feeding of the Five Thousand (Miracle of loaves and fishes) from the Methodist Church Collection of Modern Christian Art © Trustees for Methodist Church Purposes, used by permission of Trustees of the Collection
Jose B. Ruiz/naturepl.com: 99
Kaadaa: 105 (top)
NASA: 47
National Gallery: 118
Peter Schouten, *Homo floresiensis*: 93
The Da Vinci Code front cover used by permission of The Random House Group Ltd

United Kingdom: Folens Publishers, Waterslade House, Thame Road, Haddenham, Buckinghamshire, HP17 8NT.
Email: folens@folens.com

Ireland: Folens Publishers, Greenhills Road, Tallaght, Dublin 24.
Email: info@folens.ie

Editors: Dawn Booth, Daniel Bottom
Layout artist: eMC Design Ltd, www.emcdesign.org.uk
Cover design: Neil Hawkins, www.ndesign.co.uk
Cover image: iStockPhoto
Illustrations: Nigel Chilvers

First published 2008 by Folens Limited.

Every effort has been made to contact copyright holders of material used in this publication. If any copyright holder has been overlooked, we should be pleased to make any necessary arrangements.

British Library Cataloguing in Publication Data. A catalogue record for this publication is available from the British Library.

ISBN 978-1-85008-214-9

Contents

UNIT 1

Wicked!

In this unit we consider whether there is such a thing as good and evil. We investigate the sort of things that cause suffering and examine religious responses to it.

1.1 Examine what we mean by words such as 'wicked'.

1.2 Look at the connection between evil and suffering.

1.3 Find out why Christians think evil and suffering exist in the world.

1.4 Examine what Jesus did and said about evil in the world.

1.5 Consider a completely different understanding of the existence of evil.

1.6 Study some modern evils and find out what people are doing to combat them.

Wicked!

1.1 What's bad?

Here we examine what we mean by words such as 'wicked' and 'devil'.

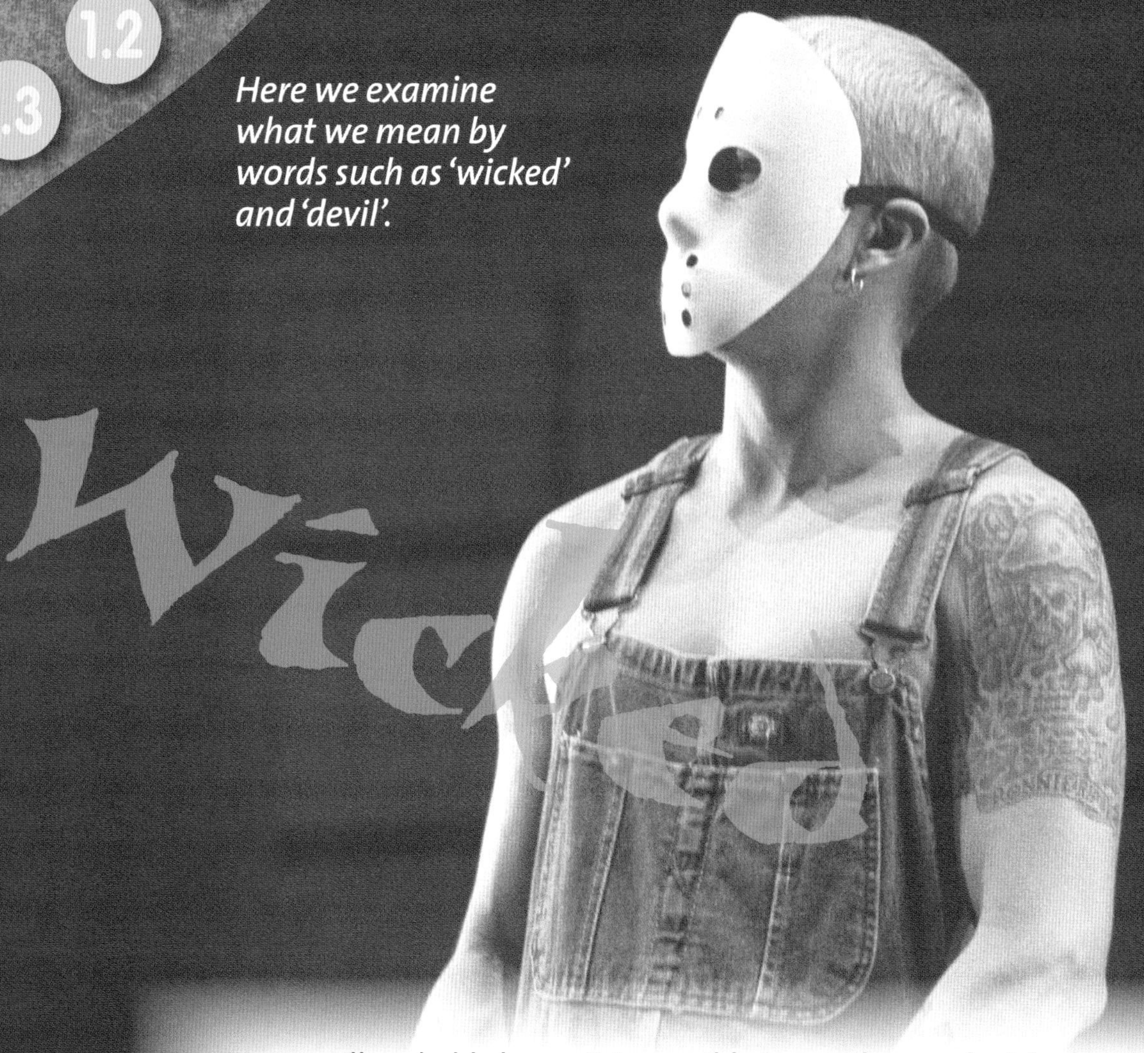
Wicked

As you will probably know, it is possible to say the word wicked and mean something terrible, then say it in another context and mean the complete opposite. Maybe it is because the idea of wickedness sounds exciting and much more fun than being good and boring. However, we do have a strong idea of what is meant by an action that is really nasty.

We also seem to possess a built-in knowledge of what is good and what is bad. If you think about it, every right-minded person in the world would agree that murder is wrong and it is evil to hurt a baby.

Husqvarna

1 *Can you think of four more things everybody would agree were evil? Where do you think we get this built-in knowledge from?*

2 *List at least eight examples of something, or someone, wicked from a film, book, computer game or the news. For example, the exploits of the boy wizard, Harry Potter, always involve his battle against evil. Against each example, explain why people would say it was evil.*

What have these things or people got in common?

3 *Some people say that focusing on evil and wickedness, as these pages do, actually encourages it rather than cures it. Do you think this is true? Why?*

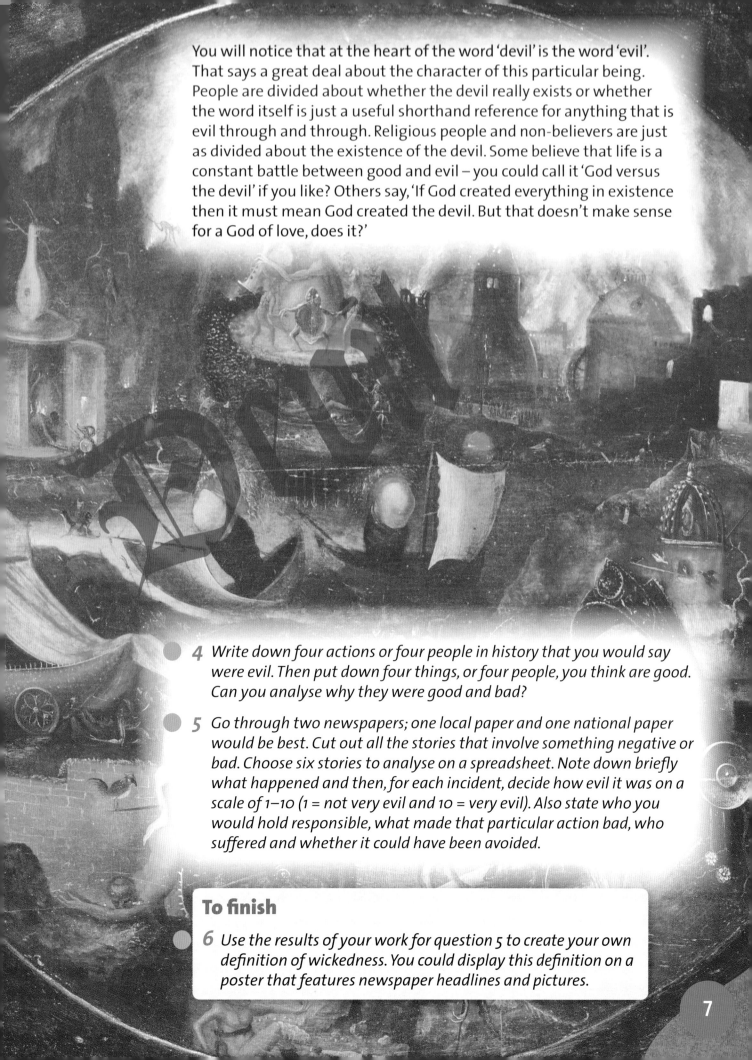

You will notice that at the heart of the word 'devil' is the word 'evil'. That says a great deal about the character of this particular being. People are divided about whether the devil really exists or whether the word itself is just a useful shorthand reference for anything that is evil through and through. Religious people and non-believers are just as divided about the existence of the devil. Some believe that life is a constant battle between good and evil – you could call it 'God versus the devil' if you like? Others say, 'If God created everything in existence then it must mean God created the devil. But that doesn't make sense for a God of love, does it?'

4 *Write down four actions or four people in history that you would say were evil. Then put down four things, or four people, you think are good. Can you analyse why they were good and bad?*

5 *Go through two newspapers; one local paper and one national paper would be best. Cut out all the stories that involve something negative or bad. Choose six stories to analyse on a spreadsheet. Note down briefly what happened and then, for each incident, decide how evil it was on a scale of 1–10 (1 = not very evil and 10 = very evil). Also state who you would hold responsible, what made that particular action bad, who suffered and whether it could have been avoided.*

To finish

6 *Use the results of your work for question 5 to create your own definition of wickedness. You could display this definition on a poster that features newspaper headlines and pictures.*

Does evil cause suffering?

Most people would say evil and suffering are closely connected. Let's examine this idea.

The destruction of the World Trade Center in America, known as 9/11, is regarded by most of the world as an evil action. Why? What do you think made it so evil?

Why do people suffer?

This is a question that has occupied people's minds for centuries. The huge loss of life caused by events such as 9/11 or the Boxing Day tsunami in 2004 raise exactly the same questions, although the causes were very different. The photographs you studied on the opening pages of this unit show that the answer is a difficult and complex one. It is because, as humans, we are reasoning beings that we try to make sense of things. An animal that is suffering is unlikely to be asking questions about why this is happening or who is to blame.

SUFFERING

DELIBERATE: In some cases, suffering may be caused by the deliberate evil actions of a person or people.

ACCIDENTAL: On occasion, there are no obvious reasons, or a person, to have caused an event where people have suffered.

NEGLIGENCE: Some incidents of suffering could have been avoided if someone had taken more care. Although a person did suffer, it was never intended.

ACT OF GOD: When suffering can't be explained. Insurance companies refer to such events as 'Acts of God'.

1 *Look back at the work you did on newspaper articles in the last lesson. Are those incidents adequately covered by the categories above? Do you want to add another category?*

Who is to blame?

When you clearly know that a person has caused suffering then you are likely to think of them in terms of evil. The victims of 9/11 were innocent people injured and killed by the deliberate actions of others. An abused kitten gets into that state as a result of human action. It may have been deliberate cruelty or simply neglect but both are wrong and some would say evil.

Acts of God?

When passengers in a car are killed by a tree falling on them in gale-force winds, whose fault is that? Who is to blame for the earthquake and tsunami wave that killed 300 000 people in 2004? You might say people were responsible for the car accident because someone should have cut down a dangerous tree. Earthquakes and lightning strikes are harder to blame someone for. In fact, insurance companies call them 'Acts of God' when someone tries to claim compensation. What an insurance company means by this strange religious expression is that they won't pay out because no human can be held responsible for what has happened. Do you think God is responsible or is it just fate?

To finish

2 *Write the script of a radio debate between Chris, who says evil is caused by people, and Sam, who says suffering is just one of those things that can't be helped.*

1.3 The Christian response to evil

Here we find out what Christians think about the existence of evil and suffering in the world.

Why does evil exist?

Most Christians agree that evil occurs because humans don't obey God's will. This is explained in Genesis, the first book in the Bible, where Adam and Eve, the first human beings, are thrown out of the Garden of Eden for deliberately doing what God told them not to do. Whether this was a real event or just a story doesn't affect the message that disobeying God is wrong and is the cause of unhappiness. Christians believe that evil was introduced into the world by people, not God. Evil continues to exist today because people still do wrong.

This picture of Adam and Eve shows the traditional Christian belief for the existence of evil.

What's the problem?

While Christians can explain how evil began, they find it difficult to understand why a God who loves his creations should allow it to carry on. Look at it this way: if God is so powerful, why doesn't he just destroy evil? Could this mean God isn't powerful enough? Or maybe he doesn't want to. There is another problem too. If God created everything, then he must have created evil. Why would he do that? These questions have caused Christians problems for centuries.

1 *What would you say was the reason for terrible things happening in our world?*

Any answers?

One traditional Christian explanation of evil involves the existence of the devil. Satan, as he is sometimes called, is believed to be an evil figure who rules over hell and spends his time tempting people to come and join him. There are many stories about how the devil came to exist. One story says that Satan began as a good spirit but became jealous of God and then turned evil.

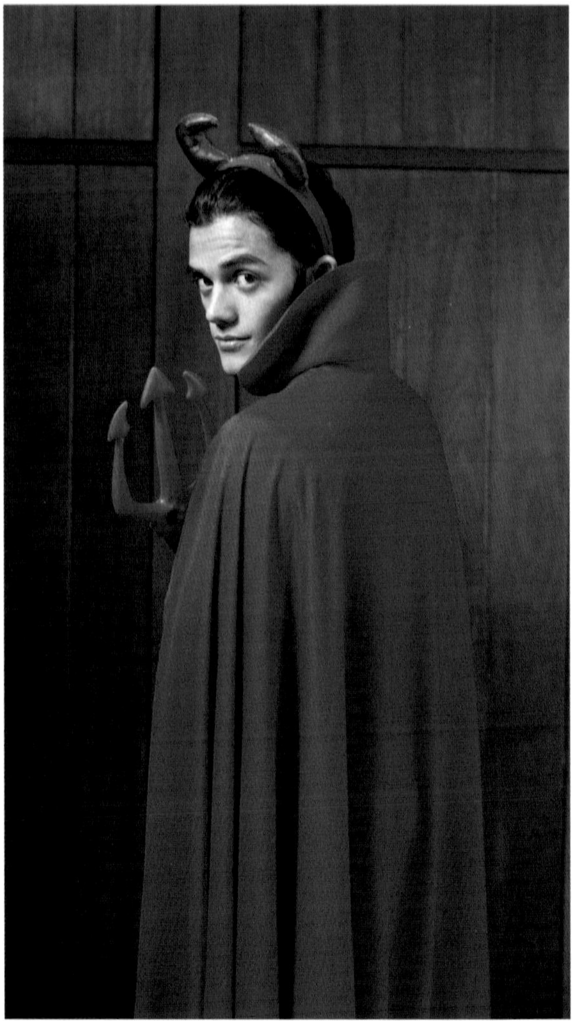

The costume in this picture is often associated with the devil. It is a bit of fun but not everyone regards Satan and evil as harmless fun.

Not all Christians believe that evil is a devil figure. The key to understanding evil, they say, goes back to the Adam and Eve story. Evil is not caused by God but by people. Because none of us are perfect, we make mistakes; that leads to evil and suffering.

It's a test

The bravery someone shows when faced with illness can make them a stronger character in the end. Or the wealthy person who suddenly loses all their money may come to realise what life is like for poor people. Although the experience was painful, they may come out of it as a kinder or more generous person.

Some people believe suffering is God's way of testing and helping them to develop into stronger individuals. It is not just those who are suffering who are being tested either; the way in which people help those suffering is also a test. Since Christians believe God knows exactly what they are thinking and doing, they will be rewarded accordingly in the afterlife.

Another important argument for the existence of evil hinges on the fact that we are free to choose what we do. Humans are not programmed like computers. We have free will and can decide what we do. That means we are just as free to do evil things as we are to do good things. Now you can't blame God for that!

To finish

2 *Draw a spider diagram with EVIL in the centre. Put the various reasons that Christians give for the existence of evil around it. Put a different score, on a scale of 1–10, (1 = not very evil and 10 = very evil) against each one, to show how you rate each argument.*

Jesus' battle against evil

Christians learn about evil and suffering by studying how Jesus, the Son of God, responded to them.

What did Jesus say?

In fact, Jesus didn't spend much time talking about evil. His was a more positive approach, teaching people what they ought to be doing in life rather than what they shouldn't. However, his teaching included stories that give Christians guidance on tackling evil.

The parable of the Good Samaritan (Luke 10:25–37), demonstrated how wrong it is to ignore a person who needs help. Because the person who did help came from a group of people who were looked down upon, the story also highlights the evil of racism.

What did Jesus do?

'Actions speak louder than words', they say. So Christians pay great attention to what Jesus did during his lifetime. In Luke's Gospel (4:1–13), Jesus comes face-to-face with the devil. There are no red horns and forked tail here, just a tempting little voice urging Jesus to show off and win supporters that way.

1 *Read the story of Jesus' encounter with the devil in Luke Chapter 4.*

   List the three things the devil wants Jesus to do and then state how Jesus handles them.

2 *Write a blog by the devil, telling of his encounter with Jesus and why it was unsuccessful.*

3 *In pairs, make up a story in which evil is a tempting little voice urging a 20 year old to do wrong.*

Jesus' reaction to the evil of pain and suffering was to heal the person.

There are other references to Jesus' encounter with evil spirits when he was healing people. One incident reported in Luke's Gospel (9:37–43) was when Jesus met a boy who was suffering from fits. The boy's father called out to Jesus to help him.

'I beg you, look at my son – my only son! A spirit attacks him with a sudden shout and throws him into a fit, so that he foams at the mouth; it keeps on hurting him and will hardly let him go! I begged your disciples to drive it out, but they couldn't.'

Jesus asked the man to bring his son forward.

'As the boy was coming, the demon knocked him to the ground and threw him into a fit. Jesus gave a command to the evil spirit, healed the boy, and gave him back to his father. All the people were amazed at the mighty power of God.'

Today it is unlikely that many people would think the boy's illness was caused by evil spirits. Medical evidence points to this being a case of epilepsy. What is significant for Christians is that, faced with this suffering, Jesus immediately took steps to help the boy by removing the evil that had plagued his life. Following Jesus' example, modern Christians believe it is their duty to try and relieve suffering.

4 *We may be surprised to see such an illness referred to as having evil spirits behind it, but it is not unusual to hear cancer referred to as one of the evils of the twenty-first century. Explain why people think of cancer in these terms. Give two ways that Christians could help in the fight against cancer.*

Jesus overcomes evil

Jesus' most significant action relating to evil and suffering involved his own death. He was faced with unjust accusations, then torture and execution; all for something he hadn't done. Christians believe that Jesus accepted a cruel death and then rose from the dead in order to show that he had beaten the evil and wrong that bad people had brought into the world.

Remember

Christians believe that by giving his life, Jesus paid the ultimate price for the evils of humanity.

1.5 The Hindu view of evil

Here we examine a completely different understanding of the existence of evil, from the perspective of the Hindu religion.

Evil is natural

That might seem like a controversial statement to make and one which might open the floodgates to all sorts of issues. It does, however, sum up the Hindu attitude towards evil. Hindus believe that life is made of opposing forces such as: good and evil; dark and light; birth and death. That doesn't make evil acceptable, but for them it solves the question that Christians have been struggling with – namely, 'Why does evil exist?'.

The god Shiva

Hindus believe that there is one god, the Supreme Spirit, but that God has many different facets, like a cut diamond. To help worshippers understand this, there are many gods each showing a different face of the Supreme Spirit. The god Shiva is one of the three most important gods in Hinduism and he combines the contradictory forces of good and evil.

This image of the Hindu god Shiva shows a balance between the power of good and evil.

Shiva is shown as the creator and the destroyer. In one of his hands he often carries a drum, symbolising the 'big bang' – signalling the beginning of the universe. Another hand will often carry the flame of destruction. Creation (which we think of as good) and destruction (which we think of as bad) can be closely linked. You only have to look into the life cycle of the Jack Pine tree, which grows in North America. Its habitat is subject to forest fires but it is these fires that breed life. Fire provides the trigger for the cones to open and release the seeds to germinate. So fire may be an evil destroyer, but it can also create life.

The destruction of these slums makes way for the creation of clean, modern housing that will bring good to many people.

1 *Make a list of four things that we rely on that involve or require fire (think as widely as you can, for example a petrol engine relies on a spark to work).*

2 *Give two of your own examples of destruction leading to something new and good.*

It's all part of life

Hindus do not think that God is the source of evil. They believe that evil occurs when God is absent or people are unaware of God's presence. We can all think of terrible things that have happened to someone when they don't seem to have deserved it. It might be a baby who loses the battle for life through illness, or a kind, caring person who seems to have a run of bad luck. Hindus have no difficulty in understanding why things like these happen. They believe it is all to do with karma. All actions have consequences. According to the law of karma, everything we do makes something else happen. Some things we do cause good and some cause harm. (See *REflections 1*, pp. 34–35.)

Hindus, who believe in reincarnation, also believe that an action in this life will have repercussions in our next life on earth. For example, a baby that suffers may have built up a bad karma in a previous existence. Equally, the person who always lands on their feet no matter what they do may have built up a good karma in their previous life.

3 *Tell a story that involves bad karma. In other words, the consequences of a person's action that result in evil happening to them later.*

To finish

4 *Create a diagram, or write two paragraphs, showing the difference between the Hindu and Christian ideas of evil.*

1.6 Fighting modern evil

Evil can take many forms in the modern world. Here we consider some of these forms and what people are doing to fight them.

Does evil really exist?

The idea of red devils with forked tails tempting us, or people fighting evil monsters, is certainly the stuff of myths and legends. This has led to some people dismissing evil and wickedness as old-fashioned or total fiction.

Some people are convinced that evil is a real force in the world today as much as it ever was and that it just shows itself in different ways. One definition of evil is that it is the absence of good, rather than being a thing in itself.

Some people argue that no person is 100 per cent evil. There will always be a part of their personality containing a spark of kindness. The greatest villain might have a soft spot for his family or take care of an elderly friend. By appealing to their good side, some argue, it is possible to defeat evil. Do you think that is possible?

Modern evil

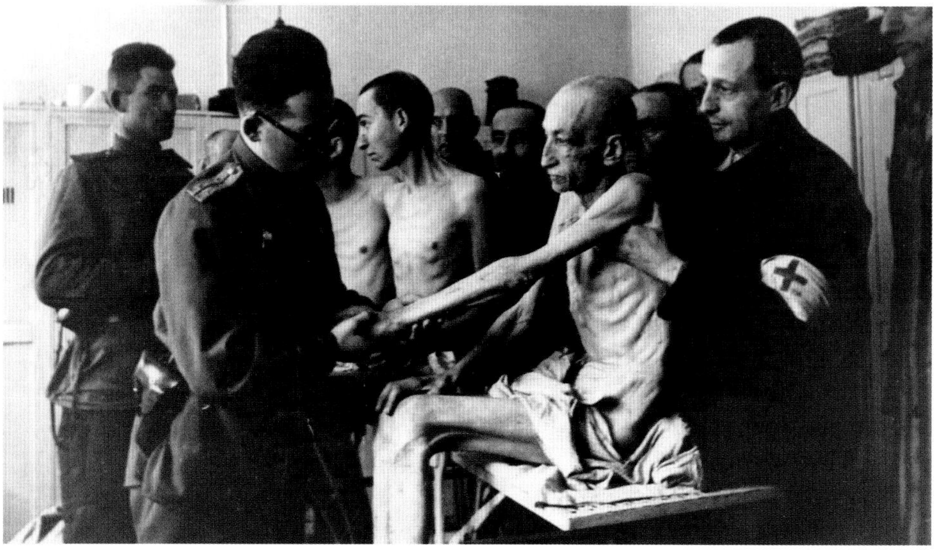

Scenes like this, when the death camp Auschwitz was liberated after World War II, convinced many people that evil does exist.

Many people regard terrorism and wartime atrocities as proof that evil still exists today. It is hard to argue that the death of 6 million Jews during World War II, on Hitler's instructions, was anything but an example of pure wickedness.

Many people regard Dr Harold Shipman as a totally evil person. He murdered at least 215 of his patients. The fact that he killed the very people who trusted him to make them better made his actions especially wicked.

'For evil to prosper, all it needs is for good people to do nothing.'

This was the message of an eighteenth-century philosopher. Interestingly, if you agree, then it makes us all responsible for the continued existence of evil. Do you think that is fair?

1 *Make up a story that would explain the meaning of the statement to a ten year old. Try setting it in the playground.*

2 *Is that statement true when you consider the examples of Hitler and Harold Shipman? Can you suggest any action people could have taken in either case to have stopped these two evil people?*

3 *Write a piece for a charity's fund-raising presentation that explains why some people say this photo is a representation of the existence of evil in the modern world. Make sure you give some indication of who you think is responsible.*

Christian Aid

This charity is in no doubt that it is evil to stand by and do nothing about the suffering in the world. It supports many projects designed to help people get back on their feet.

There is a project in South Africa to help people grow the aloe vera plant and make face creams to sell. Another helps people make and sell herbal medicines; not only does this bring in money for poor families but it also eases some of the devastating effects of HIV in the area.

To finish

4 *Visit the Christian Aid website (www.ChristianAid.org.uk) and look at the ways this charity is trying to defeat modern evils. Report to the class on the project that impressed you most and explain why.*

1.7 Picture this!

This woman points to what is left of her home after an earthquake.

1 *Explain how each of these images might be connected with evil. Do they meet your definition of evil and wickedness from 1.1?*

The carcase of an elephant left by ivory poachers.

C
B
A
NO
YES
X

These people are playing on an ouija board. They are trying to contact dead spirits. A bit of harmless fun, evil or plain silly?

1.7

1.8 Just to recap

1.9

All through this unit of work we have been thinking about the concept of evil. We have considered whether there is such a thing or whether in fact it is just the absence of goodness. We have also examined the difference between the Christian and Hindu views of evil.

> *Let's remind ourselves of what we have learned:*

We began by working out what we mean by evil and its connection with suffering. **A** Why can the word 'wicked' mean both good and bad things? **B** How can evil be linked to suffering?	**We went on to look in detail** at the Christian understanding of suffering and the impact of Jesus' words and actions. **A** Give one explanation Christians might offer for the existence of evil. **B** Name one way that Jesus tackled evil.
We considered the Hindu interpretation of suffering. **A** What is the meaning of karma? **B** What is the connection between good and evil, according to a Hindu?	**We examined** the forms evil and suffering can take today. **A** Give an example of a modern-day evil. **B** Why do some people say nobody can be 100 per cent evil?

At the start of this chapter, we used the word 'wicked' in a light-hearted way but, as we worked through the units, the tone became more serious. Review your own attitude to wickedness now that you have completed the study.

This picture was used previously in 1.5 to show how destruction can lead to the creation of something good. What evils do you think poor housing can cause?

Choose one of the following tasks to check your progress in this unit.

Task one

a *What is the connection between wickedness and suffering?*

b *Why should Christians concern themselves with evil and suffering?*

c *What do you think about the ideas that nobody is totally bad and everybody has some good in them? Can you always appeal to someone's good side?*

Task two

a *Name two things that you would call modern evils.*

b *Explain why Hindus say 'evil is just a part of life'. How does that differ from the Christian view of evil?*

c *'If you suffer, it is just fate. That's all there is to it.' Do you agree with this statement? Why?*

1.9 Something extra

1 *Choose a situation (real or imaginary) where you think something evil happened and write a blog as if you were the devil.*

5 MONTHS ON,
THE GUN LOBBY
CAN BREATHE A
SIGH OF RELIEF.
EMMA CAN'T.
Emma Crozier, aged 5, was murdered by a lawfully owned gun at Dunblane Primary School on 13th March 1996. Join SAGE and help campaign for the abolition of private gun ownership.
Call Free: 0800 317938 · http://www.sage.org.uk
FACE THE FACTS. BAN THE GUN.

2 *Many people consider gun crime as one of the major evils in modern society. What do you think makes this a worse evil than many other crimes? Do you think Christians have a responsibility to do something to alleviate this particular evil? Why? How?*

3 *Think about the idea of 'wickedness'. Write down the colour, sound and plant you would associate with it. Do the same for the idea of 'goodness'. You may prefer to display your thoughts visually as a poster of two halves.*

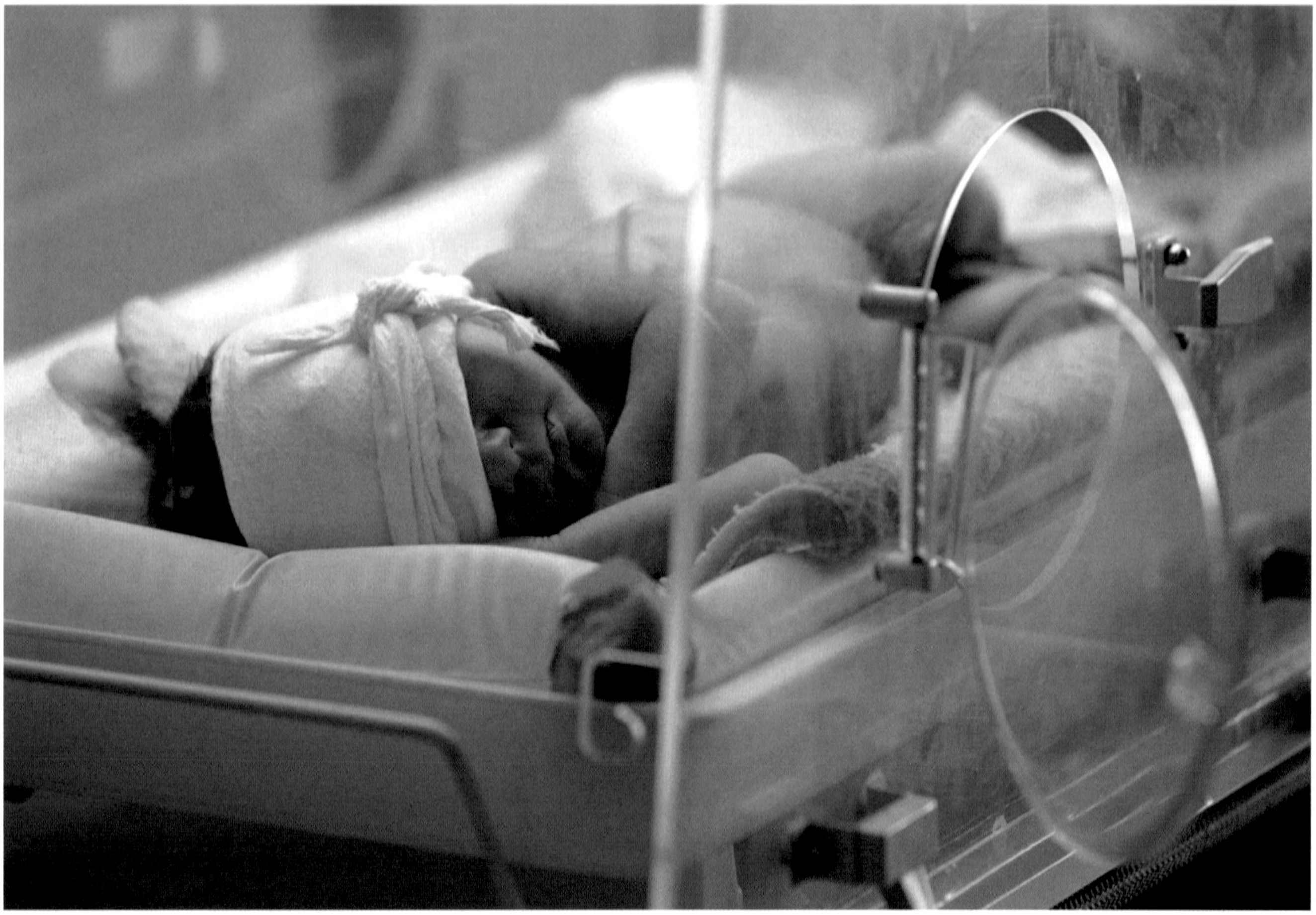

4 *What different ideas might be put forward to explain why this baby is suffering? Which, if any of them, would you agree with?*

5 *Plan a campaign for a Hindu charity (or another religion of your choice) aimed at members of the faith, encouraging them to donate money to help victims of a severe flood. You will need to remind yourself how the religion regards suffering. Your campaign requires a leaflet to be distributed at the place of worship, possibly along with a poster.*

6 *Create your own poem about 'goodness'. It could take the form of an acrostic or haiku poem or a simple one with only one verse.*

7 *Find out what Muslims believe the reason for human suffering is. Present the results of your research to the class and tell them whether the Muslim view is close to either of the other two religious attitudes we studied in this unit.*

8 *Reply to Cassie's email, which she sent to a teenage magazine. In your answer, try to present both sides of the argument before summing up with your own opinion.*

'I think it's stupid the way people go on about magic and the occult being wicked. It's just a bit of fun and can't do any harm. Where's the problem?'

Cassie (by email)

UNIT 2

Humans are special

In this unit we examine what sort of things make human life precious and worthy of preserving, and look at different attitudes towards the intervention of medical science.

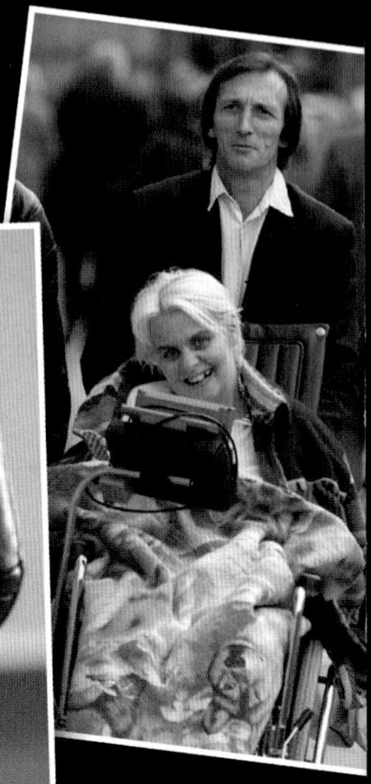

2.1 Consider what it is that makes human life so special.

2.2 Think about the point at which a foetus becomes a person.

2.3 Ending a life is traumatic. We weigh up different views.

2.4 Consider the controversial issue of euthanasia.

2.5 Examine in detail the arguments for separating conjoined twins.

2.6 Look at different reasons why people want to choose the baby they have.

Humans are special

2.1 Life is precious

Here we look at the way people and religions regard human life as something extra special.

Life is sacred

You have only got to think of the great lengths the emergency services go to in order to save someone's life, to realise that human life has great value. Strangely, in a situation like this, it doesn't seem to matter whether people believe in God or not; we all value human life and go out of our way to preserve it.

1 *Draw a speech bubble on a piece of paper. Inside it, write why you think people go to great lengths to save a life.*

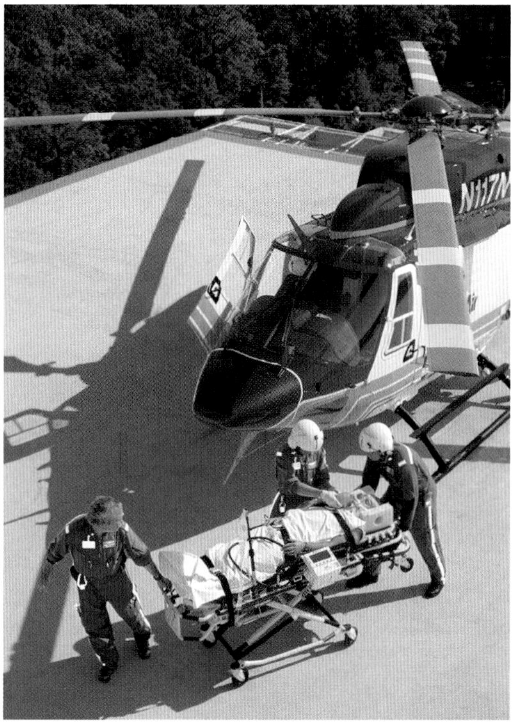
N117M

Why spend so much money trying to save one life when there are billions of people in the world already and more born every second?

'I think life is a gift from God. We are clever and can grow human tissue in the lab and all that, but we can't create life from nothing. Only a super being like God can do that. None of us can arrange when we are born, nor when our life will come to its natural end. It is all in the hands of God. That is the reason I treat life with great respect.'

'Just because I don't believe in God, it doesn't mean I don't value human life. I do. It is because I think this is the only life we have that I set great store by it. I am a Humanist. Reason and experience lead me to think human life has a special value and I believe leading a happy and fulfilling life is what matters most.'

2 *Draw a chart to compare these two views of human life. What do these people agree about? Where do they differ? Which of these views is closer to your own? Add a further sentence to explain your own personal view.*

The Bible says:

> *'God created human beings, making them to be like himself.'* (Genesis 1:27)

> *'Don't you know that your body is the temple of the Holy Spirit, who lives in you and who was given to you by God? You do not belong to yourselves but to God.'* (St Paul's Letter to the Corinthians 6:19)

Sanctity of life

Christians use the expression 'sanctity of life' to describe their belief that human life is precious. 'Sanctity' means 'holy' and shows that Christians believe human life is a gift from God. Some also interpret the phrase to mean that a person's life belongs to God. You can see both ideas in the biblical quotations above.

If you think about these ideas for a moment, you will realise they have implications for what you can do with your life.

3 *Write down what you think a Christian might say if you asked them their view on suicide.*

4 *Write the extract from St Paul (above) in your own words.*

5 *Use the two passages above to write a paragraph explaining why Christians believe human life is sacred. You will need to include biblical reasons in your answer.*

What is the Muslim view of human life?

Muslims believe that Allah creates life: he chooses the moment when we are to be born and then breathes life into us. Life is a gift from Allah. It is not ours to do with as we wish; our life is on loan to us from Allah. The Qur'an states: 'No one dies unless God permits. The term of every life is fixed.' (3:145)

To finish

6 *Script an interview with one of the paramedics in the picture, on page 26, who is a Christian. What reasons might he give for choosing this career?*

2.2 When does life begin?

It is easy to accept that a baby is a person but exactly when does a cluster of cells become a person? In this chapter we examine different people's views on this subject.

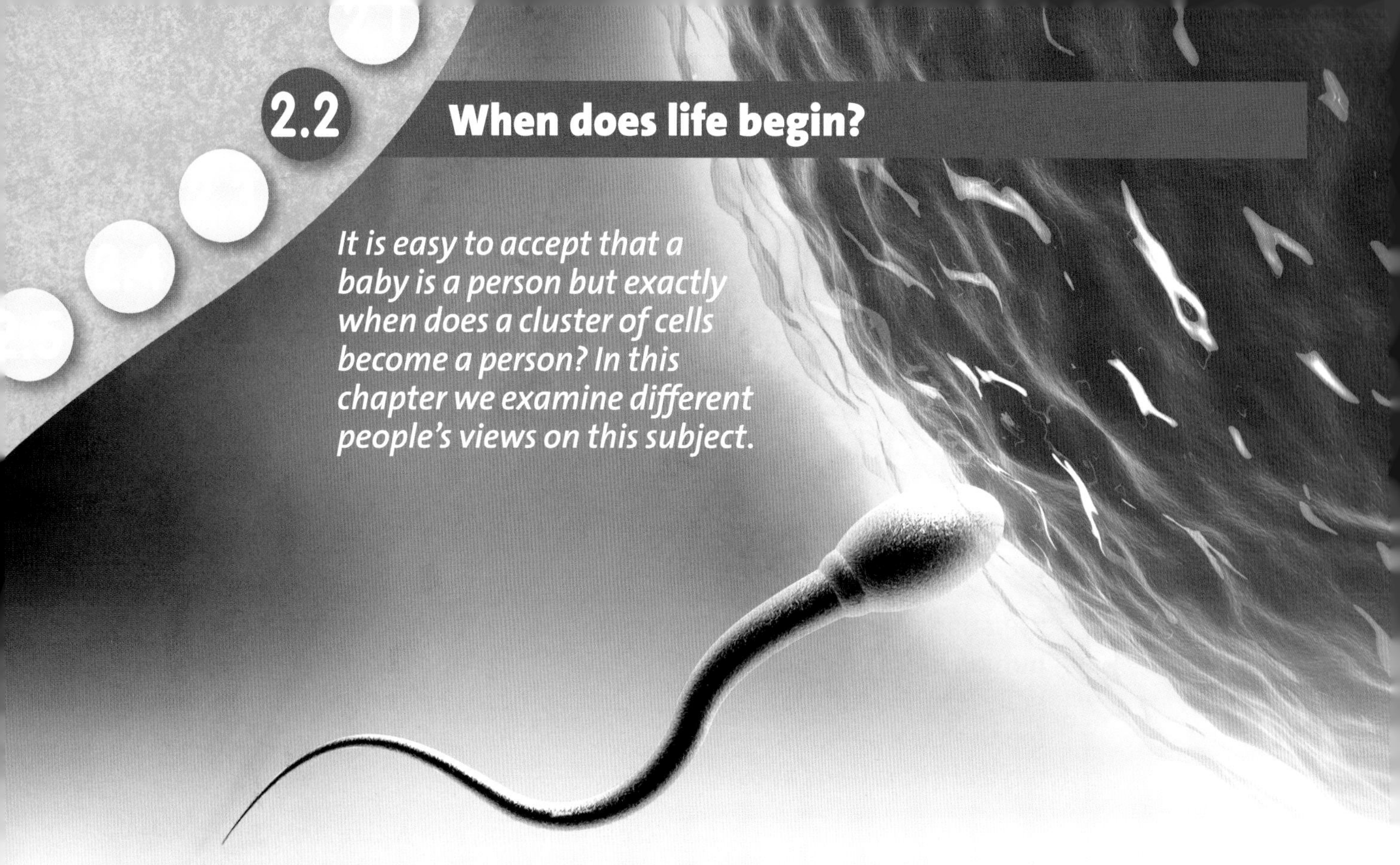

This is the moment when a sperm fertilises an egg to create a foetus.

Do you think life begins at conception?

The picture above captures the precise moment when one of thousands of sperms reaches an egg to fertilise it. From then on, the egg has a unique DNA that becomes the personal 'ID' of an individual for the rest of their life. No one else is exactly the same as this person, even though there are 15 billion people in the world.

1. *Discuss: Would you say that this picture shows the moment life begins? If this is the beginning of life, what implications does it have for using the morning-after pill?*

The Roman Catholic Church says fertilisation is the moment that life begins. It argues that every child is a gift from God and 'from the first moments of his (her) existence, a human being must be recognised as having the rights of a person – among which is the inviolable right of every innocent being to life. *(Catechism of the Catholic Church)*.

Those who say this is not the moment life begins, point out that it takes another seven to ten days before the egg embeds itself in the womb and another week before it is firmly attached. They believe that until that moment the foetus is simply a collection of cells, not a person.

Life begins later

Muslims believe that an individual is a foetus until it reaches 120 days of existence, at which point God breathes a soul into it, thus making it into a human being. From then on, the person in the womb has their own rights and that includes the right to life.

Others argue that the foetus doesn't have the same rights as a baby until it reaches 20 weeks. That is the time when the mother will be able to feel it kicking.

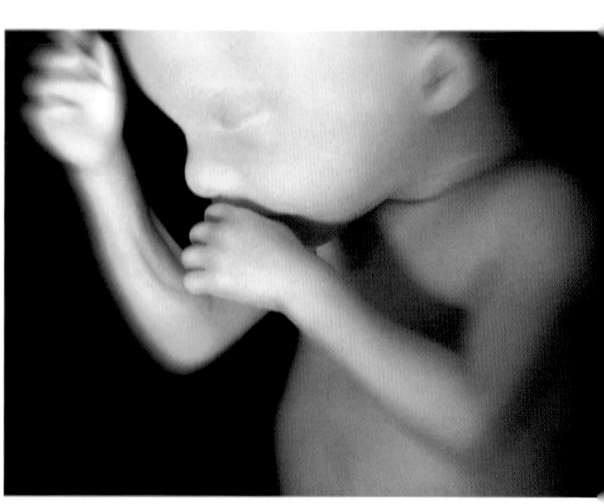

This foetus is 20 weeks old. As you can see, its limbs are already well formed.

It has got to be able to survive independently

For some, the foetus only becomes a baby when it is capable of surviving outside of the womb. Traditionally this has been at around 27 weeks. However, advances in medical science have been pushing the boundaries. A baby born in Canada at 22 weeks has survived but this is rare, and babies who survive at 24 weeks have an 80 per cent risk of being disabled.

'Every life is precious. That means everything possible must be done to resuscitate a tiny baby even if it faces a life with disabilities.'

2 *Write a response to the statement above, either supporting or disagreeing with it, and then explain your views.*

It's only human once it has been born

Although Judaism recognises that a foetus is a unique individual, this religion does not agree that a foetus has equal human rights as its mother until the baby is halfway out of the birth canal. If there was a medical problem, where the mother's health was at risk, her life would take priority over the survival of her unborn child.

To finish

3 *A production company has been asked to produce a television programme called 'It all begins here'. Outline to the presenter the difficulties of deciding at what stage a foetus becomes a person. Tell the presenter when you think a person's life begins and why.*

2.3 Abortion

Ending a pregnancy is a traumatic decision for all concerned. Here we look at different views on abortion.

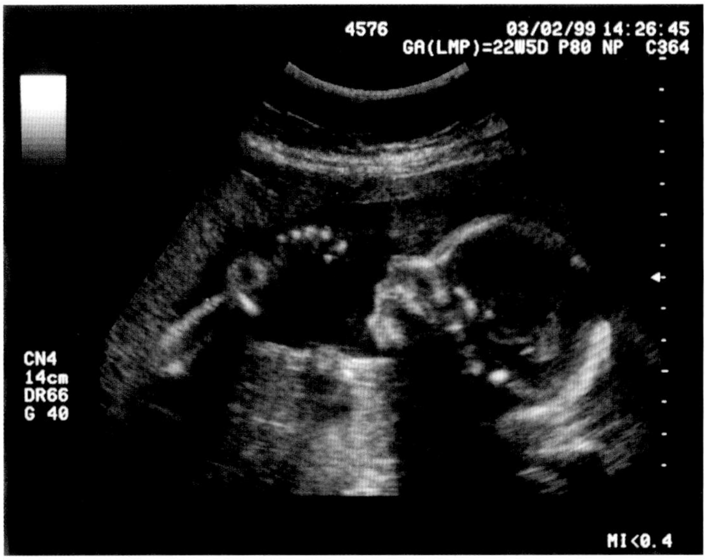
4576
03/02/99 14:26:45
CN4
14cm
DR66
G 40
MI<0.4

Do you see this as the first photograph of a new person or simply the computerised image of a foetus?

Bloggers R Us!

I worked hard at my GCSEs and I was doing my AS subjects when I got pregnant. We certainly didn't plan it and I thought we had taken enough precautions. Clearly we hadn't. Jake was chuffed though. He thought it would be fun to have a baby while we were young. I'm not sure though. It means I can't go to uni now, doesn't it?
I can't decide whether to have an abortion. Jake says no. He doesn't agree with things like that. He says it's murder but he's not having the baby. He also says that he has got as much right as I have to say what happens to the baby. Has he?

I am already ten weeks gone now and I have got to make a decision. What should I do?

Chloe

Consider these different responses to the subject of abortion:

A lawyer says: 'Abortion is legal if two doctors agree a mother's physical or mental health is at risk. The operation must be carried out before 24 weeks.'

A statistician says: 'On average, 500 abortions are carried out every day in England alone.'

A doctor says: 'My training was aimed at saving life, not destroying it. I have known premature babies of 23 weeks survive in intensive care. Scans also show the foetus making walking motions at 12 weeks.'

The Catholic Church believes: The human being is to be respected and treated as a person from the moment of conception – 'a person ...' is entitled to '... the inviolable right of every innocent being to life'.

A pro-choice campaigner states: 'It is my body, my life and my decision either to have an abortion or to keep the baby. Nobody else has the right to tell me what to do.'

A Christian believes: 'You must not commit murder and that is what abortion is.'

The Baptist Union, who believes in the sanctity of life, says: 'There is a recognition that taking life may be the lesser of evils in situations of rape, incest and particular threat to the well-being of the mother, the foetus and the wider family.'

1 *Choose two contributors from above with opposing views and write their response to Chloe's blog. Each needs to state their view about what she should do and give their reasons for this opinion. What would you advise Chloe to do?*

Who is entitled to have a say?

Chloe's blog highlights the difficulty she is having in making a decision about an abortion. It is also clear from what Chloe says that she is not the only person who is involved. Her boyfriend, Jake, is mentioned. There could also be others she hasn't mentioned such as her Mum and Dad, whose grandchild this is. There is also the doctor who might be asked to perform the abortion.

To finish

2 *Create a mind map of the various different people who might become implicated in any decision involving an unborn child. You might want to put the foetus as one of them. It doesn't have a voice but should its rights be considered? When you have created your mind map, link the people together so it is clear who you think is at the heart of this decision and who is on the periphery.*

2.4 The right to die

Some people believe that if a person is seriously ill they have a right to end their life with dignity. Others think that is totally wrong. Let's consider the difficult issue of euthanasia.

Euthanasia

Euthanasia is sometimes referred to as 'mercy killing'. This is because it involves deliberately ending a person's life, either because they have requested it or because it is thought to be the kindest thing to do. For example, we make these decisions for our pets. An elderly cat or a dog that is very ill may be 'put to sleep' because it is thought they are suffering. While most people think this is right for an animal, public opinion is sharply divided when it comes to humans. Euthanasia is illegal in most countries around the world.

Those who agree with euthanasia argue that a very ill person should have the right to end their life and, thus, their suffering. Those against euthanasia say that life is precious and should never be deliberately ended, even if a person requests it. There is always the possibility that a cure may be found for their illness.

Christians believe that human life is a gift from God to be preserved and nourished. They do distinguish between killing someone and allowing them to die naturally. This means doctors should not be forced to keep someone alive.

Muslims believe that God has a plan for everyone's life which we cannot understand. Suffering might be part of God's test and it is wrong for anyone to take life, even their own.

Think carefully about the Christian statement above. There are two parts to it. Belief in the sanctity of life means Christians firmly disagree with 'putting a person to sleep' as though they were an old dog. They do, however, say that a person's life should not be prolonged artificially just for the sake of it. That means they would permit doctors to switch off a life-support machine if it was clear the patient would have a poor quality of life.

1 *Write a reply from a Christian doctor to a request for euthanasia. He needs to state the law, what he was taught (see page 31), as well as his religious views.*

The hospice movement

Euthanasia is not the only solution. The first hospice was set up in the 1960s by a Christian woman who wanted to provide care for terminally ill patients. These are people suffering from incurable illnesses. The hospice provides love, care and support for the patients and their families. Drugs are used to control pain and help the people during the final days or months of their lives.

2 *'Hospices are places of life not of death', said a doctor. What does he mean by that?*

CASE STUDY 1

Diane Pretty brought the issue of euthanasia to public attention in 2002. She suffered from motor neurone disease and, as her illness progressed, was faced with the prospect of a painful death. Diane asked the British courts to allow her husband to help her commit suicide, without him being prosecuted for murder. She was so incapacitated by then that she was unable to end her life herself and needed help. 'I want to have a quick death without suffering, surrounded by my family so that I can say goodbye to them', she said.

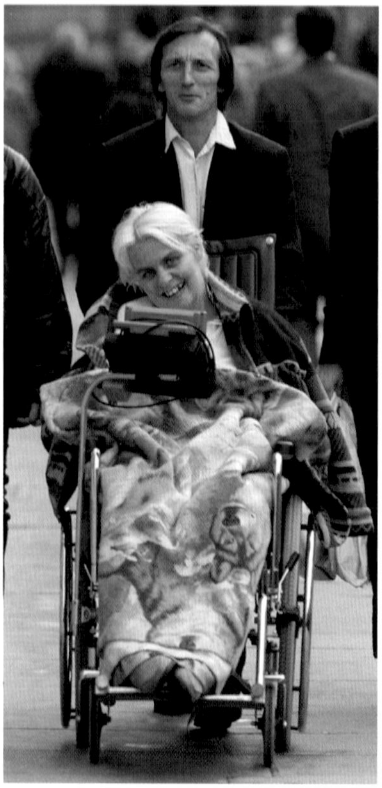

The court refused. So, for ten months, she battled through the courts right up to the European Court of Human Justice but eventually lost her case. She died in a hospice where she was cared for during her final days.

3 *Why do you think no court would permit this?*

CASE STUDY 2

Jan Grzebski, aged 65, made the headlines in 2007 when he awoke after 19 years in a coma. He was knocked unconscious by a train in 1988, while working on a railway in Poland. He was not expected to live more than two or three years. His wife nursed him at home and did her best to include him in family events. When he eventually came around, he had hazy memories of being taken to family gatherings and of members of his family trying to communicate with him.

4 *What does this case study add to the debate?*

To finish

5 *There are many conflicting views on these pages. Consider the different arguments and display them in a diagram or explain them in writing. What is your view?*

Having studied some of the religious arguments about the sanctity of life, we ask how much medical science should intervene in the natural course of human life.

WHAT IS THE RIGHT THING TO DO? YOU DECIDE!

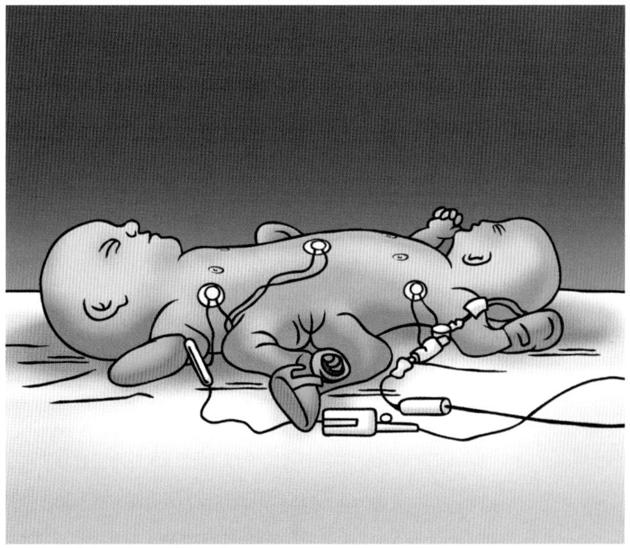

The High Court has been asked to decide on the case of Jodie and Mary (not their real names), conjoined twins born at a Manchester hospital with their spines fused and abdomens joined. Their parents are strict Christians and believe that only God can give life and only God can take it away. They believe it is wrong for doctors to intervene in their daughters' lives. Surgeons at the hospital say that without treatment both girls will die because it is Jodie's heart and lungs that are keeping both twins alive. Eventually the strain will drain Jodie of life. Doctors believe Mary has only primitive brain functions compared with Jodie.

Surgeons want the court's permission to go against the parents' wishes and separate the twins. The operation, which is expected to last 20 hours, would give all the major organs to Jodie. There are risks involved for Jodie and she would need many more operations and skin grafts during her life. Mary would die immediately.

1 Who should decide what the right thing to do is?

- *The parents*
- *The doctors*
- *The church*
- *The court*
- *The girls themselves when they are old enough*

Go through each of the above and give your opinion about why they should or shouldn't make the final decision.

The newspaper account you have just read, on the previous page, was a real life case that caused lots of discussion in 2000. In the end, the Court decided that doctors must ignore the parents' wishes and operate to save Jodie and let Mary die. You can read more about this case by looking at the BBC's website (www.bbc.co.uk) or one of the major newspapers' websites. You will also be able to get an up-to-date account of Jodie's life since the separation from her twin – her real name is Gracie Attard.

2 One person on television said, 'Doctors shouldn't play God. It can't be right to kill one person to save another.' What did they mean by that and what would you say in response?

Although we have considered religious arguments about the sanctity of life, there is no easy answer to this dilemma. Jodie and Mary's parents, who were Roman Catholic, prayed about the problem and decided they should leave God to decide who lived and who died. Their mother said later she feared that even if Jodie was given life, she might spend her life in a wheelchair and suffer deformities.

Some Christians argued that life is precious and people should try to save it if possible by giving Jodie the chance of life. The problem, of course, is that it meant condemning Mary to death.

3 Write a blog that you think Jodie might write as a young teenager when she looks back on the decision that gave her life instead of her sister.

To finish

4 Jodie's parents have said they want to tell her the truth about what happened at some point. Write a letter to Jodie's parents giving your views on this and, if you agree, suggest what would be the right age and how they should explain it to her.

2.6 How far should science go?

Advances in medical science mean that it is now possible to carry out a large number of procedures that were not previously feasible. Let's consider whether we feel that such advances are a good thing.

Just because you can do it, it doesn't make it right

Medical science advances at a rapid pace and many things are now possible that were never dreamed of. This has raised many questions about what is right and what is wrong as people fear that scientists may go too far. At the same time, many things that we are grateful for and accept as normal today raised fears in the past.

Louise Brown, born in 1978, was the world's first 'test-tube baby'. Her conception was the result of IVF.

Assisting couples to have a baby is one area which raises lots of concerns. Pioneering work on IVF treatments, which involves collecting women's eggs from their womb, fertilising them with sperm in a laboratory, then planting them back in the wombs, worried many people at the outset. Today it is a routine procedure that has helped more than a million women worldwide have children.

Right or wrong?

Designer babies

Should couples be able to choose the sex of their unborn baby?

Some people are concerned that if parents can choose the sex of their child, it will reduce the value of human life to little more than choosing a new pair of trousers. Unwanted embryos of the wrong sex are destroyed. Is this right?

1 *Besides personal preference, what other reason might someone have for wanting to choose the sex of their baby? Do you think that is acceptable? Why?*

Transplants

When surgeons began heart transplants, some people thought that it was wrong because traditionally our heart is the seat of our emotions. People often say, 'I love you with all my heart'. What happens if you have got someone else's heart? Although early heart transplants were not very successful, techniques have improved and today patients go on to enjoy a good quality of life as a result of this operation.

2 *Should we be allowed to transplant any body part? There have been face transplants but what about brain transplants? At what point does someone become a different person?*

There have been experiments transplanting animal organs into humans to help with a shortage of donor organs.

3 *Why might a Christian refuse to have an animal organ transplant? (Look back at the teachings on page 27.) Would you consider it?*

Genetic engineering

Once DNA was discovered, it became possible to extract genes from one living being and replace them with genes from another. It is possible to put genetic material from a spider into a strawberry. In the plant world there have been scare stories about genetically modified crops but attempts to use such crops for good have also continued; for example, apples have been grown with antibodies in order to help prevent tooth decay. Some experiments have concentrated on genetically manipulating animals so that their milk contains antibodies – which would also help humans.

4 *How far would you allow genetic engineering to go when it comes to manipulating animal life?*

To finish

5 *Choose one area from the spider-gram to investigate further and present your findings to the class or in a leaflet.*

- *You need to research what is currently happening in this field. The Internet can give you up-to-date material.*
- *Find out what the advantages and disadvantages of this issue might be.*
- *Choose one religion and examine its teachings on the sanctity of life. Investigate its current views on this sort of procedure.*
- *Give your own views at the end.*

Picture this!

BAN
VIVISECTION
MURDER
FOR PROFIT
aLV.org.au
VIVISECTION
MURDER
FOR PROFIT
aLV.org.au
BAN
ANIMAL
TESTING
aLV.org.au

- *Write a comment on each of these pictures, highlighting what it has to do with the idea that 'humans are special'. Remember that the picture may actually be implying the opposite and challenging the statement!*

2.8 Just to recap

All through this unit of work we have been asking why human life is precious and worth preserving. We have thought about issues concerned with the beginning and the ending of life. We also considered how far medical science could intervene to alter the natural course of a person's life.

Let's remind ourselves of what we have learned:

We began by looking at why religious people and those of no religion both think human life is special. **A** Why might an atheist believe human life is precious? **B** Give one reason why Christians think that human life is sacred?	**We went on to look in detail** at different ideas about when life begins and people's attitudes to abortion. **A** When do you think life begins? **B** Why would some Christians be against abortion?
We considered whether people have a right to choose when they want to die. **A** What is meant by the word 'euthanasia'? **B** Why do religious people (and some people with no religious beliefs) think euthanasia is wrong?	**We went on to examine** the difficult decisions some people have to make about medical treatments and using scientific research. **A** Which advances in medical science would you say have helped us the most? **B** Which area of modern scientific research do you think is the most controversial?

At the start of the unit we discussed the idea that human life is a precious commodity worth saving. Which areas of study did you find the most interesting?

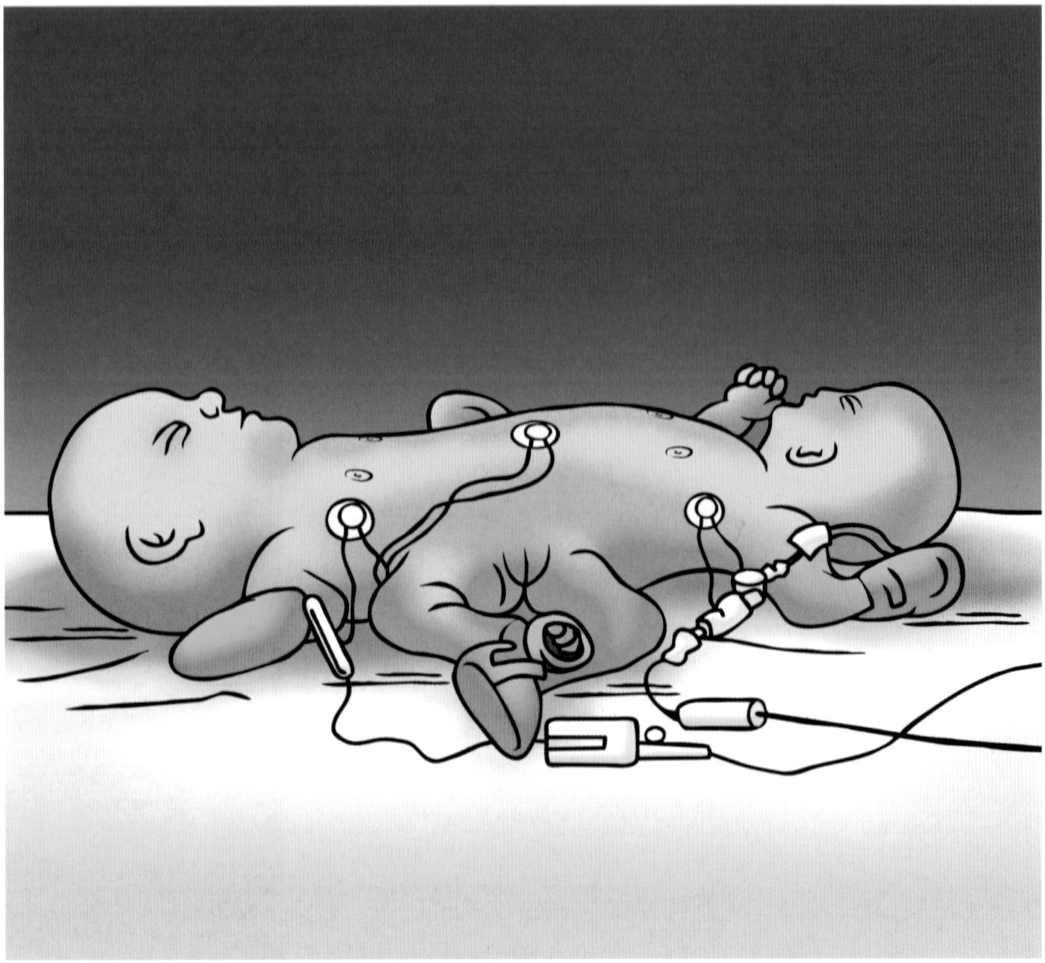

Write down the different issues the case of Jodie and Mary raised. If you were a parent, would you be prepared for experts to make decisions about the future of your child? Why?

Choose one of the following tasks to check your progress in this unit.

Task one

a *What do people mean when they say that life is sacred?*

b *Explain why a Christian or a Muslim would not believe that euthanasia was right?*

c *'Everybody has the right to decide things for themselves.' Would you say that this statement was true when it comes to abortion and euthanasia? Why?*

Task two

a *Why is euthanasia such a controversial subject?*

b *Explain some of the different ideas about the moment when life begins. When do you think we should consider a foetus to be a person?*

c *'If life is so precious then no expense should be spared to save it.' Would you agree with this statement? Why?*

2.9 Something extra

1 *You have been asked by a children's hospital whether it ought to support research into developing pigs with organs that might be suitable for transplanting into humans. Write a letter to the hospital management giving your own opinion. Also tell them what you think members of some religious groups might think about this and why.*

2 *Write a caption to the picture on the right explaining why the issue of abortion creates such strong opinion. You will need to show that there are two sides to this argument.*

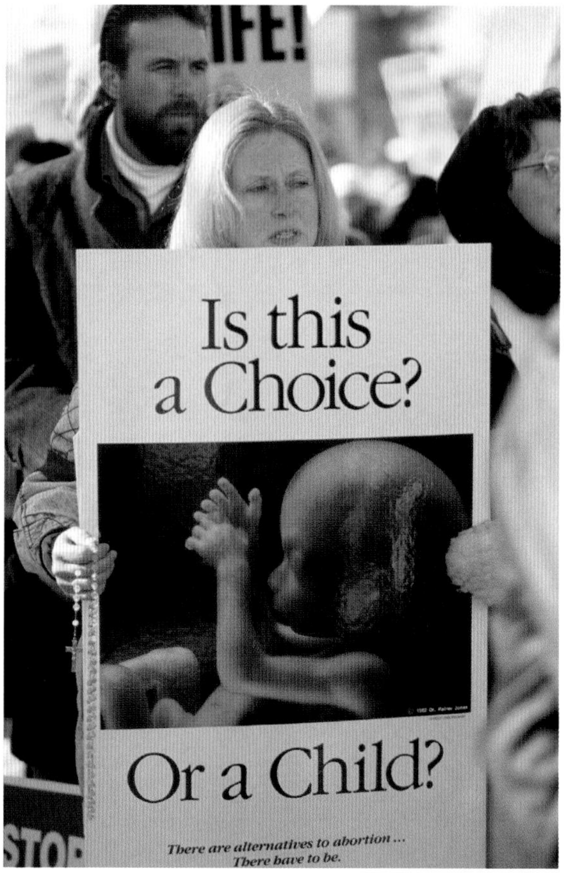

Is this a Choice?
Or a Child?
There are alternatives to abortion ...
There have to be.

An anti-abortion march.

3 *Read through the following real-life cases and give your advice to the people concerned, backed up with reasons. The reasons may be drawn from a religious teaching, based on something you have seen or heard about, or just your own opinion.*

CASE STUDY 1

The Hashmi family from Leeds asked to have permission to select a male embryo from various fertilised embryos produced by IVF treatment (see page 36 if you need to remind yourself what this means). The male embryo was to be placed in Mrs Hashmi's womb to develop, so she could give birth to a baby boy. The family needed its next baby to be a boy so the blood from his umbilical cord could be used in a bone marrow transplant to save the life of the eldest son, Zain. There had been a worldwide search for a suitable match for Zain and his last hope was the blood from a brother.

4 *Would you allow a baby to be created purely to save the life of another child?*

Use the BBC's website (www.bbc.co.uk) to find out what the outcome of this case was.

CASE STUDY 2

A 64-year-old woman in India, who is married but has never had any children, asked for IVF treatment. The egg would be donated by a female relative and the sperm would be her husband's. If the fertilisation was successful, the resultant embryo would be implanted back in her womb to develop normally.

5 *Would you permit treatment like this? What do you think a Muslim might think about this case and why? (Look back to page 32 for help.)*

You could read what decision was reached in the case of Mrs Subramaniam on the BBC's website (www.bbc.co.uk).

6 *Referring to the photo on the right, explain why we don't call this creature a human or value its existence as much as a real person. It is capable of doing many things we can do and in some cases can do them better.*

ASIMO
HONDA

7 *A woman who was six months pregnant went into a French hospital and was mistakenly given an abortion. Do you think the European Court should rule that it was the death of a child or a foetus? What difference do you think it would make?*

8 *Write a page for a website that explains why some Christians support the hospice movement. You may need to research hospices in more detail.*

9 *Write your own poem that includes the line, 'Life is for living'. You could use the line as the title or the verse, if you wish.*

Life is for living

UNIT 3

Is there anybody out there?

In this unit we consider the reasons people give for believing or not believing in a higher power than themselves. We also examine the different places some people think God is to be found.

3.1 Think about the belief in, and search for, alien life forms.

3.2 Examine different approaches to the search for God.

3.3 Consider the reasons for belief and non-belief.

3.4 Look at the argument that if something exists then someone must have designed it.

3.5 Examine the reasons Christians give, and the methods they use, in the search for God.

3.6 Study the ideas behind the many images of Hindu gods.

Is there anybody out there?

3.1 Life in outer space

Many people believe there is more to life than simply what is in front of their eyes. Here we examine one of those beliefs.

The Hubble Space telescope has discovered more than 200 new planets outside our solar system. The big question is: do any contain life as we know it?

Lots of people are fascinated by the possibility that we may not be the only life form in the universe. Maybe there is a lot of difference between scientific attempts to make contact with life on other planets and people who believe in the existence of a higher being than ourselves. But both have faith in the possibility that something does exist that can't easily be seen or proved.

Science fiction?

It might seem like the stuff of science fiction to be talking about life on other planets but plenty of distinguished scientists think it is possible. Just because we haven't made contact with any extraterrestrial life forms, doesn't mean that they don't exist. In fact, a great deal of money has already been spent on the search for life in outer space.

The work of the Hubble Space telescope is overseen by the Space Telescope Science Institute in Baltimore, USA, and in 2006 the head of the space programme, Mario Livio, said, 'We are all dreamers, and part of that dream is to find life somewhere... We're finding that the galaxy is full of planets, and the chances are, somewhere out there, we will find one with the conditions necessary to be habitable.'

1 *Conduct a survey of at least 30 members of your year to find out what percentage of people believe there is life on other planets. It might be useful to record a few of the reasons they give, then you can discuss these as a class.*

Life on Mars

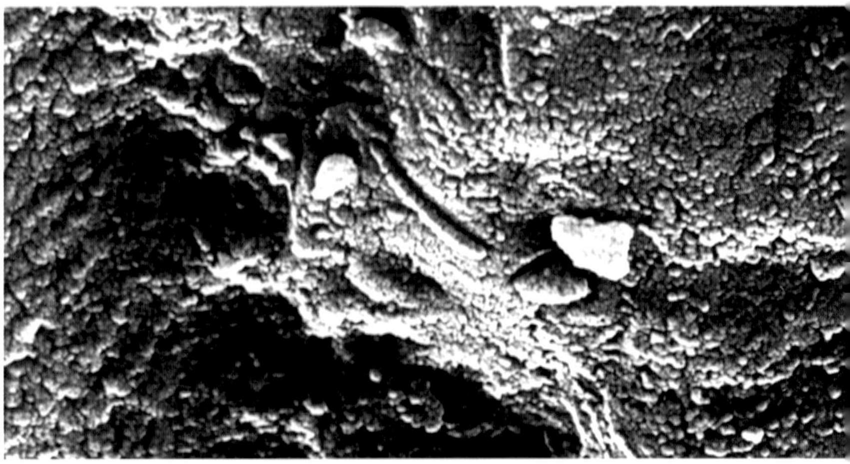

Some scientists believe that this meteorite is proof there was life on Mars because it is believed to contain evidence of fossilised bacteria.

Films and books telling stories of little green men from Mars have entertained people for years. And in 1996, NASA found a meteorite that really had come from Mars. It contained evidence that water had flowed through it and there were traces of chemicals associated with decaying bacteria. NASA scientists said this may be proof of life on Mars. However, not all scientists agree.

2 *Write an article for a newspaper about research into extraterrestrial life forms. Check the Internet for up-to-date research. Include reasons why some people think there is life on other planets, then conclude with your own views.*

Making contact

Just in case there is the chance of contacting other life forms, some of the space probes have carried data. Pioneers 10 and 11 carried plaques showing the location of the Earth in the galaxy and the solar system, as well as an outline of the human body. The Voyager probes also carried recordings of sounds and pictures from Earth.

There are some scientists who continually broadcast messages and images into outer space in the hope that someone, somewhere, will pick them up and respond one day.

People's attempts to contact the higher being they call God are similar. They trust there is someone out there who will hear their prayers and respond. But that being is far more caring than an alien.

3 *Draw a chart to show the similarities and differences between a scientific search for extraterrestrial life forms and a religious search for God.*

To finish

4 *Give your own response to this criticism: 'This is an RE textbook. What have little green men got to do with RE?'*

3.1
3.2
3.3
3.4
3.5

Where do you look for God?

People have various approaches to searching for God. Here we consider four ways of doing so.

Look in the natural world

Some people believe that God exists within the world and its beings. They don't see God as an external power but someone whose essence is found in everything in existence. Watching a flower bud unfurl, the sun setting over the ocean or a mountain range capped with snow makes them believe in something greater than themselves. Because none of these things are manufactured, some people see them as evidence of God. The idea that God exists within the natural world is one that Hindus also feel comfortable with. For them, God, who they call the Supreme Spirit, is present in everything that exists, has ever existed or ever will exist. What makes this idea intriguing is that Hindus believe the Supreme Spirit exists as much in a rock as in a mouse.

For Christians, the natural world does not contain God. It is evidence of his existence because he created it; no human did. Can you see the difference between the idea of God inside nature and God outside of nature?

Look in others

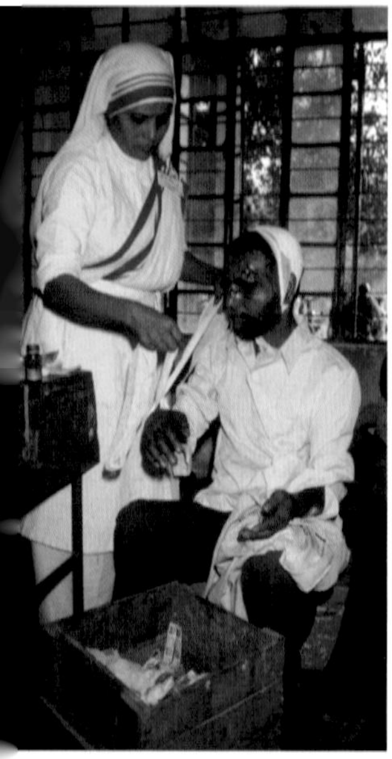

Some people look at the kindness and compassion that humans show to others in order to find God. Watching love in action helps them to understand what God is like. The kindness might take the form of something as significant as that in the photograph on the left but equally it could be a small action. It might be a thoughtful word to someone feeling down in the dumps or prompt assistance for the mum struggling to get two crying children and a buggy on the bus.

Some followers of Christianity, called Quakers, believe God is found in everybody. What is surprising is their belief that even the most hateful person has some spark of goodness within them – albeit a very tiny amount (remember page 16?)! Quakers believe that responding to this goodness, or spark of God, benefits everyone.

1 *Display the idea of finding God in people's kind actions as a poster. Use newspaper headlines and magazine pictures to make it.*

Look within

There are other people who think that if God is a spirit, then the place to look is within yourself. To do this, some people meditate. That involves sitting quietly, shutting out the distractions of life around you and thinking deeply, like the person on page 45. With practice, some people are able to understand a great deal about themselves and make sense of the world around them. For some, this enables them to gain an understanding of God. For others it means gaining a better understanding of themselves. Some people wonder whether there is any difference.

2 *Remind yourself how the Buddha put the idea of looking within yourself into practice. What did he discover?*

Look in special places

Some members of organised religions like to contact God by going to a holy place. This might be a centre of worship containing special artefacts or a sacred place like the one in the photograph on the right. Being present in a place where other believers have gathered over the years or where something special has happened, helps some people feel close to God.

The mosque is a special place for Muslims.

To finish

3 *Arrange the four ways of finding God in the order you think people might find most helpful and explain why you have ranked them that way.*

3.3 Maybe... maybe not

Here three people give reasons why they either believe in something greater than themselves, they definitely don't believe in something greater than themselves or they just aren't sure.

I am quite sure there is no such thing, or person come to that, as God. It's not like there is any evidence to prove he exists. You wouldn't normally believe something without proof, would you? No, the way forward is science. That does offer proof. I'd be the first to agree that science doesn't answer everything. But give it time. We are making new discoveries every day and eventually we will discover the answers to everything.

I'll tell you why people like to believe God exists, it's because they're scared. They like to have someone to look after them. Well get real! There isn't anyone. I am an atheist. We are on our own here and life is what we make of it! Now that is a challenge worth rising to.

I am not so sure. Let's face it, we have only got a human brain and there are plenty of things we can't get our heads around in this world. I can't visualise a black hole in space for a start! So it comes as no surprise that we can't understand the idea of a power that is greater than us.

Now I am not saying there is one. I am agnostic. I would like more proof of this power's existence. I do agree that science has discovered incredible things and will continue to do so. But, hey, I said discover. I didn't say it made them. Those things were always there in the first place, it was just that we hadn't noticed them before. So how did they get there in the first place? Now that puzzles me.

1 *Choose one of these people's arguments and list the points they make to support their argument. Which of their points do you find most convincing and which are the most questionable?*

I don't have any difficulty believing that something greater than me exists. In fact, it would be arrogant to think I am the best there is. I don't want to call this higher power God, but that is because I don't like labelling things. And once you say 'God', people get all sorts of daft ideas about wise old men. So many people in the world, from all sorts of cultures, and all through history, have believed there is something out there greater than themselves. They can't all be wrong!
The world didn't happen by accident. Let's be honest, the odds on that happening are infinitely worse than winning the lottery! So if you want to apply logic and reason to this discussion, then I'd say it obviously makes sense to believe something greater than us created the world. I am a theist.

To finish

2 *Write a script for an argument between two of these people. Remember, each person is keen to persuade the other that they are right.*

3.4 By design or by accident?

Consider whether the fact something exists is proof that somebody designed it.

UBP

This celebrity is wearing some very expensive designer clothing and accessories.

1 *Explain what you mean by designer clothing.*

What do you think it says about the person in the photograph who is wearing these garments?

What, if anything, do you think makes designer clothing and accessories different from items bought in the average chain store?

2 *You are a designer at Vision Designs and have been asked to create a new designer watch. Consider the points below:*

> We want to launch a new designer watch. Please submit a preliminary design for us to see how you're thinking.

- *Label the special features that single it out as a designer watch.*
- *What age/gender/type of person is it aimed at?*
- *How much do you think people would be prepared to pay for this designer watch?*
- *What is the unique selling point of this watch, which could be featured on advertising material?*

Amazing!

Imagine the watch you have designed slips off the model's wrist at the end of the advertising photo shoot. It falls on the grass without anyone realising. Later in the day, a person walking their dog picks the watch up. They would know this was a special watch. Not only would it shout 'quality' but it would be obvious that it had been specially designed. The finder thinks, objects like that don't exist by chance – this is a high quality designer watch.

An eighteenth-century philosopher called William Paley used a similar argument to explain the existence of God. Paley said that if someone found a watch on the ground and looked inside it, they would be amazed by its intricate works. They'd know immediately that this instrument had been designed and made by someone. They would never think it turned out that way by chance.

Cosmic designer

Paley said the same is true of this planet, which is far more complicated than any watch. He felt that the earth couldn't have been created by chance so it must have been deliberately designed this way. That means there must have been a designer. He said that the designer must be God.

3 *Write Paley's blog, telling the story of the watch and what he thinks it proves. Then write an email from someone who disagrees with him and says why.*

Paley also used this argument in relation to the human eye. He said that the workings of the human eye are so intricate that they would not have come into existence by chance: somebody must have designed the eye to be like that. The only being capable of creating something so amazing is God. That proves the existence of God, he said. But do you agree?

4 *Draw a speech bubble. Inside it, write the reasons why Paley says there must be a God.*

5 *Draw another speech bubble and, inside, write what someone who disagrees with Paley might say.*

6 *On a scale of 1–10 (1 = not convinced and 10 = completely convinced), how convinced are you by Paley's argument?*

Remember

The world we live in is intricate and amazing. For some people that is proof of an intelligent designer. They believe it is proof of God.

3.5 Where do Christians find God?

Christians have no doubt about the existence of God, so we examine what it is that makes them so certain.

Christians look to various sources to find out whether God exists. It is quite likely that someone who has been brought up in a Christian family may never question the existence of God. But, for many people, belief is a personal thing and everyone has to make up their own mind about it. Here are a few ways that Christians have come to believe in God.

Prayer

In *REflections 1*, we considered the idea that prayer was like using a mobile phone. Talking on a mobile and praying both involve the belief that there is someone there who is listening to you and who will respond. It is the response people are sure they have received to their prayer that convinces them someone was listening and cared enough to respond. That being, they reason, is God.

Through reading

The obvious book a Christian might look in to find God would be the Bible and certainly reading the scriptures has convinced many people that God exists. It is not just the Bible that has had this effect. People who have read the Qur'an and other religions' holy books have been led to a belief in God.

Non-religious books have also had the same effect on people. It is possible that works of fiction, even children's stories, have helped people understand the idea of God. The famous children's series that started with *The Lion, the Witch and the Wardrobe*, concerned with the fight of good against evil, has led some people to an understanding of God. Sometimes it can be an account of another person's experiences or search that helps.

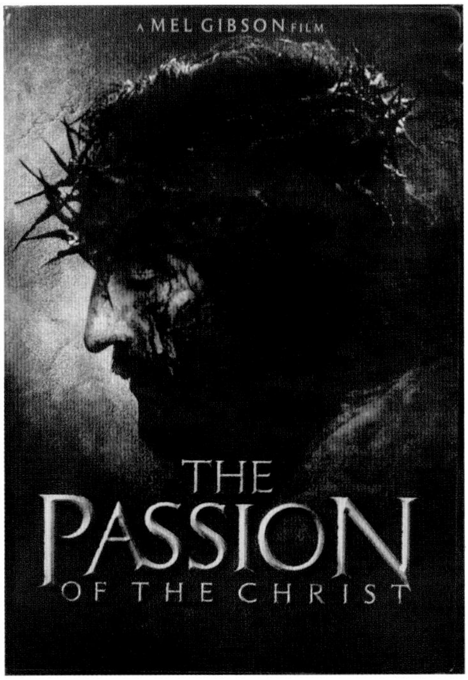
A MEL GIBSON FILM
THE PASSION OF THE CHRIST

This 2004 film, which showed the final hours of Jesus' life in horrifying detail, influenced a large number of people to consider the existence of God.

1 *Name a book or film you think might lead someone to believe in God.*

Jesus

One leading mathematician said the reason he believed in God was simply Jesus. He said there was no doubt that Jesus had existed as a historical figure and that the man's effect on history has been staggering. What is equally amazing is that the effect and teachings of Jesus are still relevant today. That, the mathematician said, could only be true of the Son of God, which in turn proves that God must exist.

Jesus said that the Holy Spirit would come to earth to help people. Christians are convinced this is true and that this spirit is evidence of the existence of God.

Other people have been convinced of the presence of Jesus in their lives. It may have been in response to an appeal for help in a desperate situation. Some have said they were only aware of the power of Jesus through experiences such as those on pages 48 and 49.

An amazing happening

On occasions, something so incredible happens to a person that it convinces them God exists. Sometimes it takes the form of healing. For example, a person who was seriously ill recovers and is then convinced that God has intervened in their life to help them.

Other Christians, and people of different religions, have had dramatic experiences in which God has been revealed to them. Such experiences are called 'revelations'.

There is an account of Muhammad's experience of God (see page 63), when the words of the holy Qur'an were revealed to him.

In Jewish and Old Testament scriptures there are stories of God speaking to Moses from a burning bush and later through thunder.

The most famous Christian encounter with God happened to Saul, who was terrorising followers of Jesus. A blinding light threw him to the ground and the voice of God was heard. The whole terrifying encounter convinced Saul he was wrong and he became a new person – the apostle St Paul.

- **2** *Read the account of Saul's encounter with God in Acts 9:1–20.*
- **3** *Write an account of Saul/Paul's experience for the local evening newspaper.*

Personal understanding

Some people arrive at their belief as a result of reading, talking and thinking about the subject. Everybody is an individual and, like falling in love, everybody's story is different.

- **4** *Design a spider-diagram poster to explain how a Christian might find God.*

Where do Hindus look for God?

Hindus have so many different images of God. What do they think he or she is like and where is God to be found?

What is God like?

The answer is actually far simpler than the picture on the right might suggest because, according to Hindus, God can look however you like! The word *like* is important. If you don't like the picture of God here then draw one you do like or feel comfortable with, a Hindu would say.

This sounds distinctly 'woolly' to people used to ideas of God, such as the Father in Christianity, or Allah, the Merciful, in Islam. As we learned on page 48, Hindus believe that God is in everything that exists. Because that means he could be in an animal, a plant, a teenage girl or even an attribute such as strength or love, they believe God doesn't have a distinct form. Now that is a mind-bender. How do you imagine something that has no form?

Faced with a picture of a Hindu god like this one, you would be hard-pushed to describe how Hindus visualise God!

1 *Write a caption that could go under the picture on this page to explain what the artist could be saying about God.*

As it can be difficult to have any feelings about a being that is formless, Hindus visualise God in whatever way they find easiest to have a relationship with. One of the scriptures says: 'The earth is my mother and I am the son of this earth.' (Atharva Veda, 12: 1–12). This means that some Hindus like the idea of a mother goddess who loves and cares for them and provides them with food. Another person might see God as someone who helps them through difficult times by pushing away problems and smoothing out their path in life.

The god, Lord Ganesh, who appears on the opposite page, is a popular deity in Hindu households. His elephant head gives him wisdom and the strength to push away obstacles.

2 *When cartoonists work, they begin by deciding the sort of impression they want their figures to create. Consider ideas such as scary, friendly, lovable, spooky, jolly and so on, then write down four words or phrases that reflect your immediate reaction to the figure of Ganesh on the right.*

This is the god, Lord Ganesh, who is a very popular image of God.

Some of the attributes of Ganesh:

- An elephant's head shows that he has the strength to push away problems.
- His large head also shows intelligence. This fits in with the idea that elephants never forget.
- He has a broken tusk and a complete tusk, showing perfection and imperfection in the world.
- His big stomach shows that he can digest whatever life has to offer.

3 *Find out what objects Ganesh is holding and what they mean.*

There are lots of ways to get from London to Glasgow

If you want to travel between these cities you could drive along the motorways or you might prefer minor roads. You could catch a fast intercity train or take the scenic route, stopping frequently and changing to local trains for each stage of the journey. The super-fit could cycle, walk or run. When it comes to it, the route you choose doesn't matter because you will get there in the end. That is how Hindus regard religion. They do not claim theirs is the only path to God. They believe that all religions lead you to God.

To finish

4 *What do Hindus mean about religion when they say, 'There are many paths up the mountain'? What is the advantage of this approach to religion? Can you spot any weaknesses?*

Picture this!

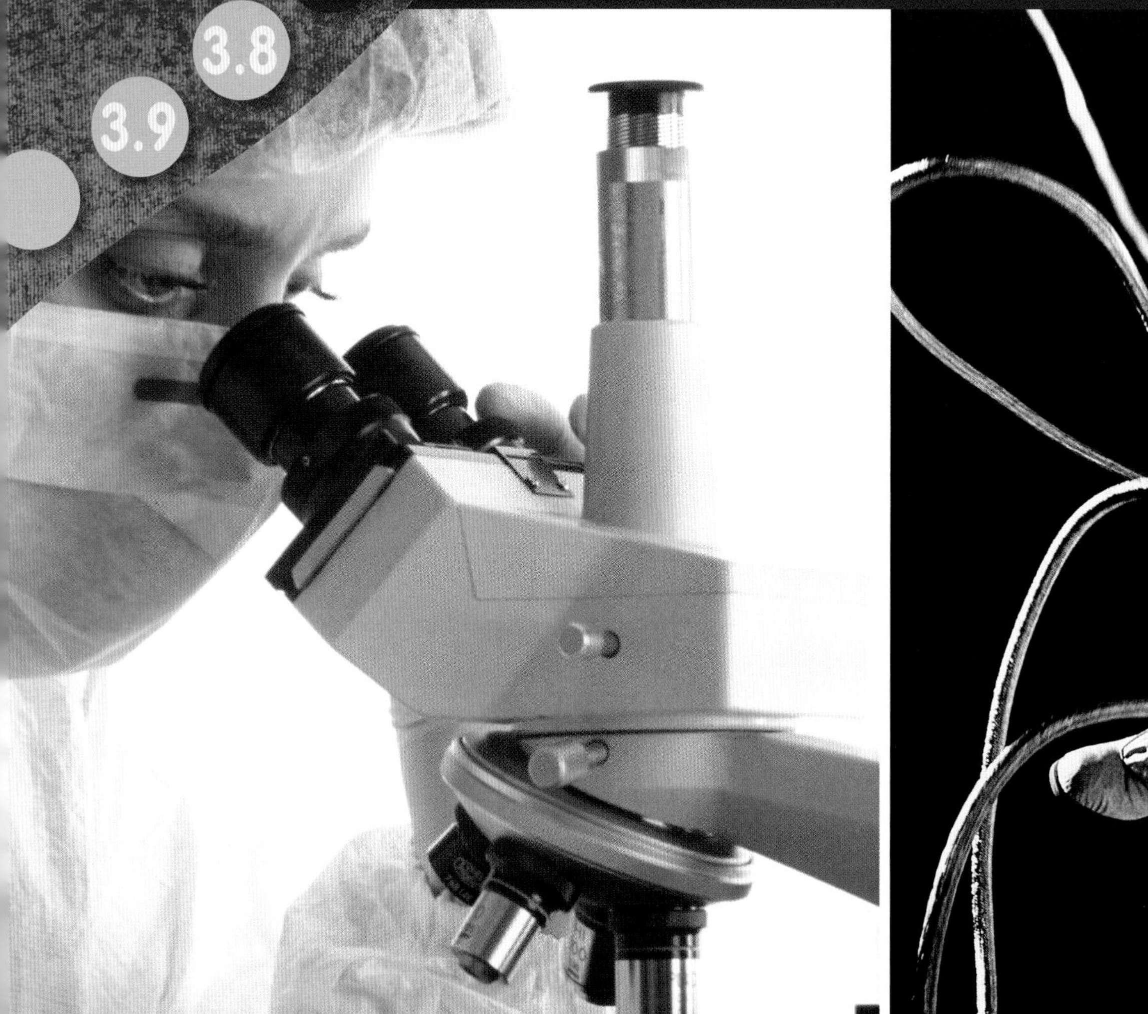

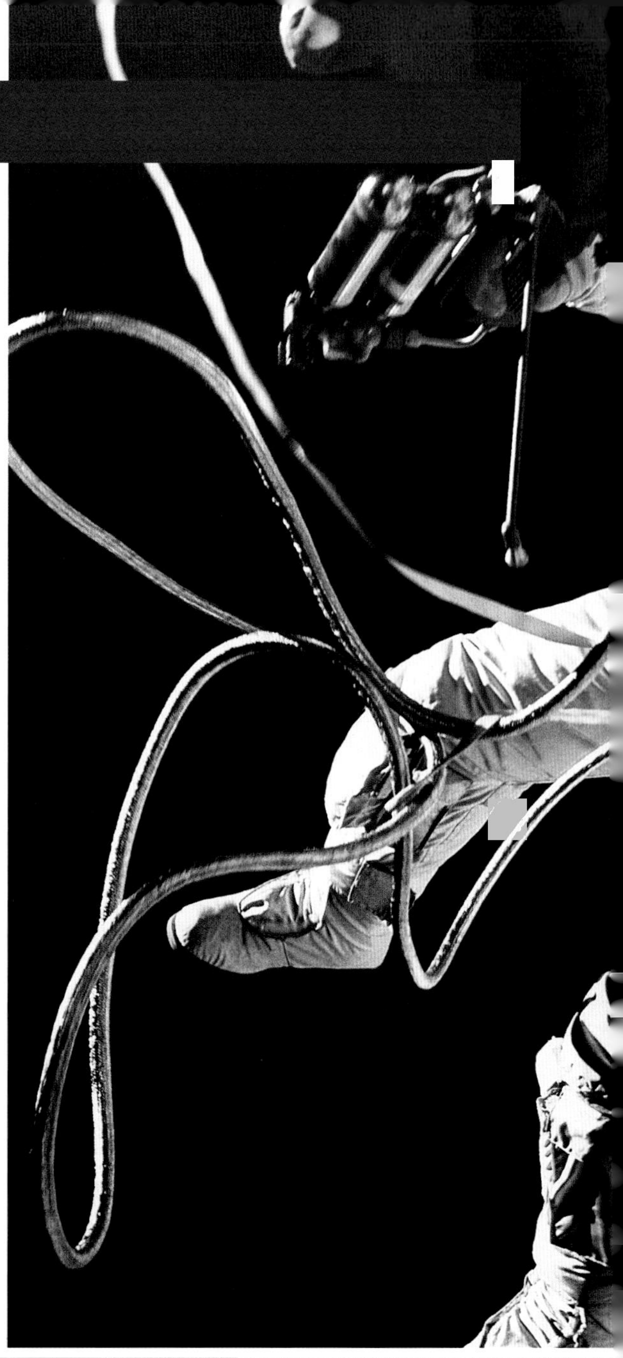

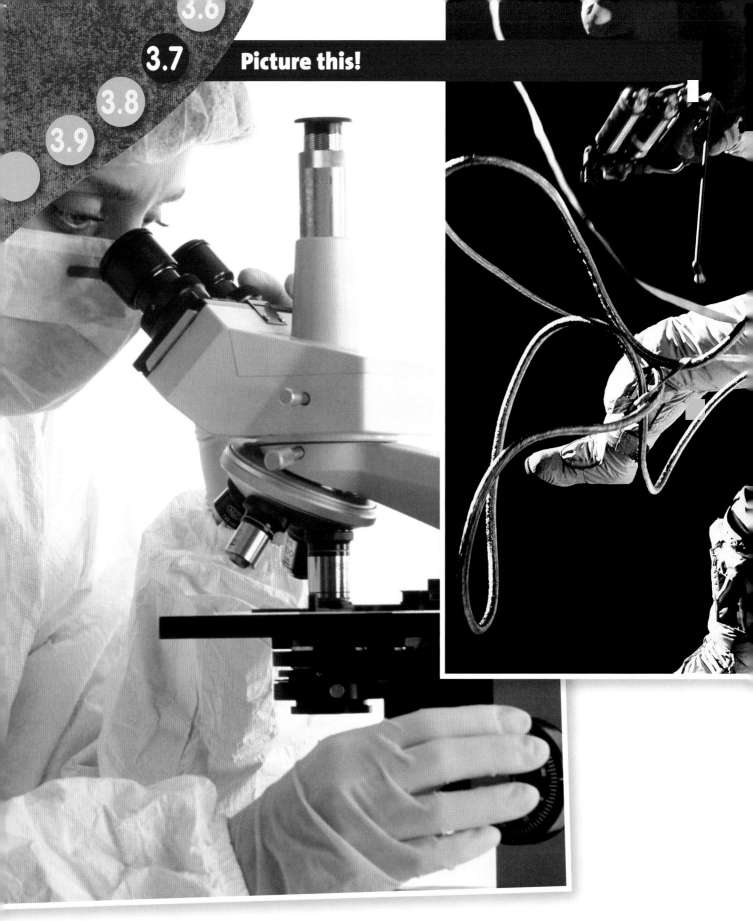

- *What is each of these pictures saying about the ways people look for God?*
- *What image would you choose to sum up your approach to this subject? It doesn't have to be one of these. It is quite possible to have an image for disbelief or uncertainty.*

3.8 3.9

3.8 Just to recap

All through this unit of work we have been looking at the reasons people give for believing and not believing in a higher power than themselves. We also examined the different places where people might think of searching for God.

Let's remind ourselves of what we have learned:

We began by thinking about belief in life on other planets and belief in God. **A** What is the connection between searching for life in outer space and searching for God? **B** What is an atheist?	**We looked** at the places where some think God can be found. **A** Name two places where people find God. **B** How does meditation help people find God?
We considered the argument that the world couldn't have occurred by accident and that God must have designed it. **A** What did a watch have to do with this argument? **B** What is meant by the idea that God is a designer?	**We went on to examine in detail** the places where Christians find God and the different Hindu approaches to God. **A** Name one way in which a Christian might be aware of being with God. **B** What do Hindus think God is like?

We started by thinking about life on other planets. Now that you have completed this unit of work, what do you consider is the best way of investigating whether God exists?

This is an image of the Hindu goddess Lakshmi. She is very popular among Hindus, who believe that she will bring them good fortune. Study the picture carefully to find clues to the way the artist has shown this aspect of God. Think about colours, the feel of the picture, things in her hand and so on.

Choose one of the following tasks to check your progress in this unit.

Task one

a *How did Paul, the Christian apostle, find God?*

b *Explain what Paley meant when he compared God to a watchmaker.*

c *How similar do you think the search for God and the search for life on other planets are?*

Task two

a *What do people mean when they say that God is in nature?*

b *Explain why Hindus have so many different images of God.*

c *Why do some people say that God doesn't exist? How would someone argue the opposite point of view?*

3.9 Something extra

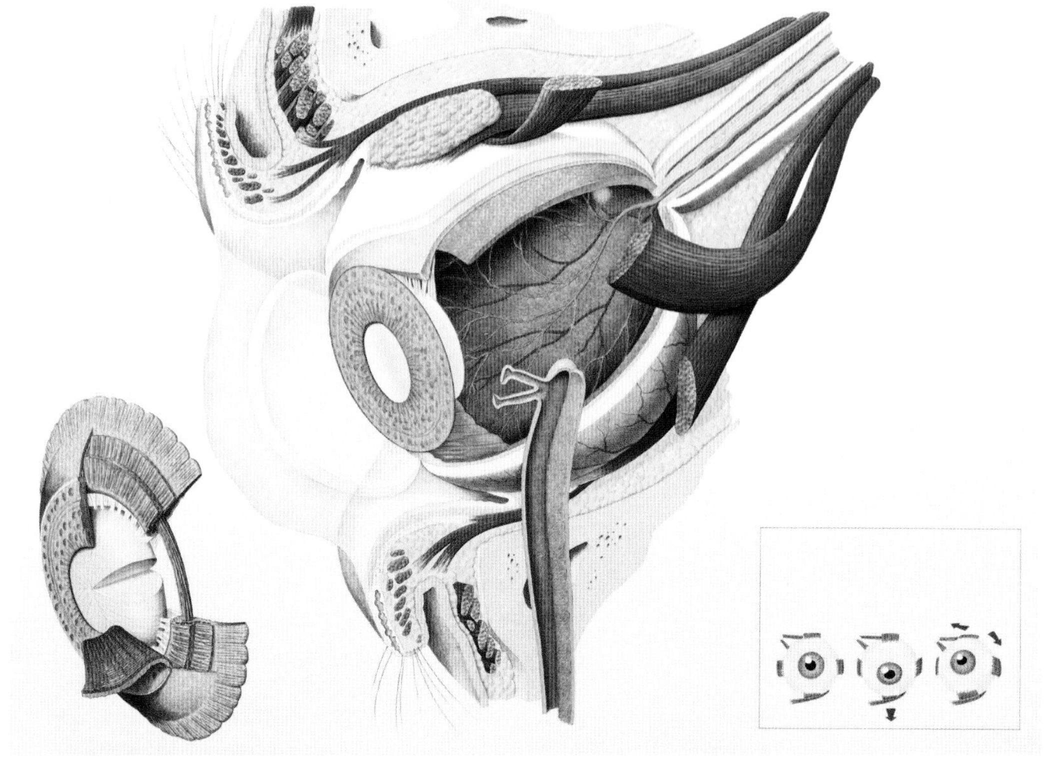

It is only when we see a diagram such as this, that the incredible structure of the eye is revealed.

1 *Someone said that if you look at the complexity of the human eye, it would convince you of the existence of an intelligent designer. Nothing so intricate could have happened by accident. Explain how this argument could be used by some people to support the existence of God. Is there anything that could be said to defeat this argument?*

2

From: JL Productions

To: Zeus Research

Subject: Pilot TV series 'The Unknown'

Message: Please present us with a plan for a three-part series to be broadcast next May. We want to include three different examples of ways that people search for something thats existence is uncertain. We definitely want one episode on religion and the search for God. What do you suggest for the others? Can you make sure the programme is fair and balanced, showing reasons for and against such beliefs?

3 *Write a blog by St Paul about his experience on the road to Damascus. You can read his story in Acts 9:1–20 in the Bible.*

4 *Design a poster to show at least three different ideas that people have about where God might be found.*

5 *Read the following extract from the Qur'an. What is it telling Muslims about the evidence for God's existence?*

'Do you not see how God drives the Clouds, then gathers and piles them up in masses which pour down torrents of rain? From heaven's mountains He sends down the hail, pelting with it whom He will and turning it away from whom He pleases. The flash of His lightning almost snatches off men's eyes.' (Qur'an, 24:43)

6 *Mother Theresa, who died in 1997, said: 'I see God in every human being. When I wash the leper's wounds, I feel I am nursing the Lord himself. Is it not a beautiful experience? I try to give to the poor people for love, what the rich could get for money. No, I wouldn't touch a leper for a thousand pounds; yet I willingly cure him for the love of God.' In your own words, explain where Mother Theresa said she found God.*

7 *Read this account of Muhammad's experience of God:*

As a young man, Muhammad seemed to have everything necessary for a comfortable life. He had married a wealthy widow and ran a very successful business as a trader. His honesty and fair dealing meant he was well respected in the community but Muhammad was dissatisfied. He felt sure there was more to life and frequently went off on his own to sit on a hillside and think. On one of these occasions he had a vision of an angel. The angel brought Muhammad words from God, which he memorised and then dictated to a scribe. For 23 years, these words were received and written down as the holy Qur'an. Muhammad was changed by this experience and went on to teach people how to live in the way God intended.

Now write a letter from Muhammad's wife to a friend, explaining what has happened to her husband.

8 *On 12 April 1961, the Russian astronaut, Yuri Gagarin, was the first man to go into space. The Russian president later said, 'Gagarin flew into space, but didn't see any God there'. Why do you think the president said that?*

UNIT 4

Miraculous! (Or is it?)

In this unit we examine some of the events that people have called miraculous and consider different attitudes towards these events and possible explanations for them.

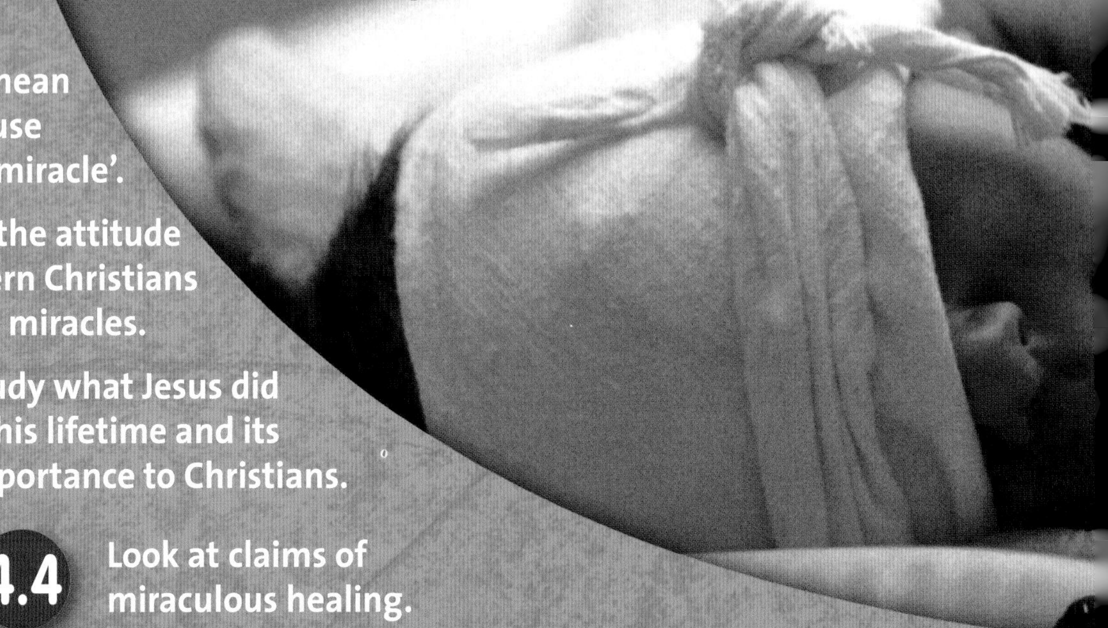

4.1 Examine what we mean when we use the word 'miracle'.

4.2 Look at the attitude of modern Christians towards miracles.

4.3 Study what Jesus did in his lifetime and its importance to Christians.

4.4 Look at claims of miraculous healing.

4.5 Examine the miraculous recovery of Jean-Pierre Bely in 1999.

4.6 Consider the attitudes of Judaism, Islam and Hinduism to miracles.

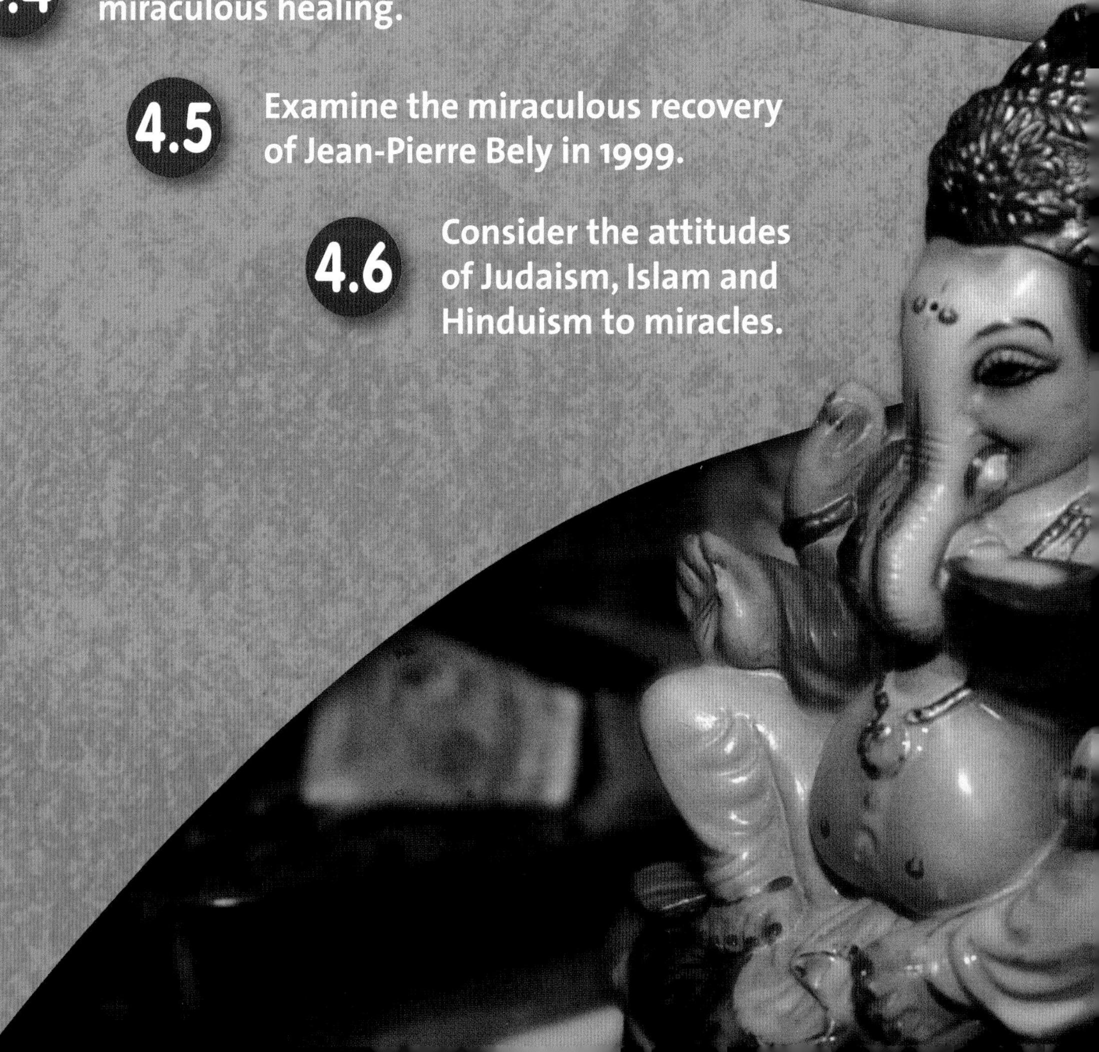

Miraculous! (Or is it?)

4.1 What do you call a miracle?

We use the word 'miracle' freely in everyday conversation, but do we all mean the same thing when we do so? What do you mean when you call something a miracle?

Geography

1 *Write your own definition of a miracle on a Stick-it note. Then stick all the class' notes on a board and discuss the different meanings. From these, work out a definition that the class agrees with.*

A miracle is something wonderful

A miracle is a supernatural event

A miracle happens when God intervenes in human life

Miracles prove there is a God

Miracles are, at best, exaggerations and, at worst, lies

A miracle is any good event that was unlikely to happen

A miracle is something that breaks the laws of nature

A miracle is just an unexpected coincidence

There is no such thing as a miracle. It's just a freak occurrence

2 *Copy the above comments onto strips of paper and arrange them in a diamond shape, with the one you most agree with at the top and the one you least agree with at the bottom.*

Here's the big question

Do you have to believe in God to experience a miracle? Usually people think of miracles in connection with religion and in the following pages we will look at what Christians believe and why. However, there are people who are convinced that miracles do happen but don't believe in God. Who then, you have to ask, is causing such phenomena? Can it simply be attributed to fate?

Have faith!

Sometimes a person recovers from a serious illness that doctors had said was terminal. How do you explain that? Did they pray for recovery and God answered their prayer? Another possible explanation is that the diagnosis was inaccurate. Let's face it, doctors are only human and they can make mistakes. Other people have suggested that the person might have healed themselves. Perhaps their determination to recover was so strong that their mind healed their body. There has been clinical evidence to suggest that this can happen. A believer might say that God works in different ways and this is one example of how he helps people to help themselves.

3 *How would you answer the eight year old who asks: 'What is the difference between magic and miracles?'*

It is all down to luck

Is it possible that some of the events we call miracles are just coincidences? The timing of an event that produces a positive outcome might seem like a miracle to the person who benefits.

To finish

4 *Write a short story containing an event that one person believes was a miracle and another person thinks was just luck.*

At certain times, the tide around this island off Northumberland is so low that you can walk across to it. Someone who didn't know this might think they were witnessing a miracle.

The Christian view of miracles

Let's look at the attitudes of modern Christians towards miracles.

How does the Church define a miracle?

The Catholic Church says that a miracle is '*... an occurrence that alters or goes against the laws of nature and is a sign of God's presence in the world. Christ promised to continue the display of miracles in his Church, but the Church admits miracles only on the basis of evidence and investigation' (The Essential Catholic Handbook: A summary of beliefs, practices and prayers, 1997: 210).*

1 Copy the above definition and underline the two most significant pieces of information that you think prevent magic tricks being accepted as miracles.

The Old Testament contains many accounts of miracles where God intervened to help people. Here, God parted the Red Sea to help the Jews escape from the Egyptians.

If the Bible is to be believed, and many Christians think it is, miracles were more common in the past. The Old Testament has lots of stories such as: Noah surviving the flood in an ark full of animals; Daniel emerging unscathed from a cage full of lions; and Moses leading his people through the centre of a sea, then watching as the water rushed back to drown his opponents. The New Testament has different sorts of miracles, which we will examine in more detail on pages 70–71.

Miracles aren't for us

Stories like these challenge religious believers in the twenty-first century because things never happen like that today. Some people say the stories weren't meant to be taken literally anyway and that they were more like Aesop's fables: stories to help earlier generations understand the existence of a powerful God. People in a non-scientific age, who wondered at rainbows, were frightened by eclipses and couldn't understand why diseases wiped out whole villages, needed stories like these. We don't. Today, we have scientific knowledge that explains why people wake up from comas or volcanoes erupt. What we require is a different kind of evidence of God's power.

What convinces us today?

The majority of modern Christians are not convinced by weird, supernatural events. What interests them is the effect that God has on a person's life. Christians do believe that God still intervenes in today's world, only in a different way. He acts through people rather than on people. A modern Christian would look for evidence of the presence of God in someone's life rather than something supernatural. Without evidence of God, there is no miracle, just a trick or coincidence, which may seem amazing at the time but it will probably be forgotten soon after.

2 *Describe the sort of incident that a modern Christian might say was the hand of God intervening to help someone. Would you agree? Why?*

What is the point of miracles?

Whilst Christians believe that miracles help people (if you think about it, you would never describe something negative as a miracle), they are sure there is more to them than that. For Christians, a miracle is likely to strengthen a person's faith in God.

3 *Write a page of text for an online encyclopaedia, explaining the modern Christian's attitude to miracles.*

Programme: The Wednesday Show

Transmission: 2nd week in June

Message: We've got a couple from Bradford on the show. They walked away unscathed when their car rolled down an embankment. They believe it was a miracle and that God saved them. Plan four questions Simon can ask to test this belief. Viewers will want to know why they think God was involved. Any idea what answers they will give?

The miracles of Jesus

The miracles Jesus performed are accepted by most Christians as events that really happened. Here we examine some of them.

Healing miracles

The miracles that often inspire Christians today are ones where people are healed. There are various accounts of Jesus laying his hands on a sick person, who promptly got better as a result. Some would argue that that is simply because they believed he would make them better – something that modern doctors call the 'placebo effect'. Drug trials have shown a significant number of people who are given tablets for an illness will get better, even when the tablets contain no medication. This is thought to be because the patient is convinced that the tablets will work and consequently their body reacts accordingly. However, it is harder to explain how Jesus could heal a person he had never met.

1 *Read the story of the Roman officer's servant in Luke 7:1–10. What does this passage say happened? If the account is accurate, what explanations are possible?*

The summer of 2007 went down in history as the wettest on record in the UK and showed how powerless we can be against the forces of nature.

Power over nature

The news today often carries frightening examples of climate change, which we cannot cope with. Perhaps the accounts in the Gospel of Jesus' miracles over nature were designed to demonstrate that this man had superhuman power; the sort of power that could only come from God.

There is a story in Mark's Gospel (4:35–41) where a strong wind threatened to overturn the boat Jesus was in. His disciples were terrified but Jesus just stood up and stopped the wind.

One alternative explanation is that from where Jesus was sitting he could see the weather changing, whereas his disciples, battling to keep the boat on course, weren't looking. They thought he had stopped it.

Some Christians believe that events happened exactly as the Bible says; others think miracle stories are just used to convey the idea that Jesus was an extraordinary person. What is certain is that Jesus made such an impression on people at the time that the stories have survived.

2 How would a man in Jesus' boat explain what happened?

Rising from the dead

By far the most miraculous story connected with Jesus is the one where he came back to life three days after he had been killed. Christians have no doubt this is true because many people saw the resurrected Jesus on various occasions. It is argued that perhaps a few of Jesus' friends may have been mistaken but it is unlikely that lots of people would have got it wrong.

Because no one in history has come back to life such a long period after their death, that makes it a miracle. In cases of near-death experiences, patients have only been pronounced clinically dead for a short time before being revived. For Christians, the miracle of the resurrection is important because they believe it proves Jesus was the Son of God.

3 Write down what a believer would say about the resurrection and what an atheist might say. What is your view?

Remember

Whether the miracles of Jesus happened or not can't be proved. It is all a matter of personal belief but they are still important to Christians because they build up the picture of an extraordinary person.

Medical miracles

One area where people today are prepared to consider miracles may happen is in the field of medicine.

When we are ill, we go to the doctor and ask for advice from someone with better knowledge than us. We have faith that they will be able to diagnose what is wrong with us and provide a solution. In most cases, exactly that happens. However, occasionally the medical profession don't know what is wrong or are unable to help. Then people are grateful to consider all types of other possibilities. That might include alternative medicines such as acupuncture or herbal remedies and there is scientific evidence showing that some cases benefit from these therapies and make a good recovery.

Prayer is something else people are prepared to consider. Some believe that asking God to help them recover may work. Factual evidence for this is mixed. One large scientific study of seriously ill patients in a Coronary Care Unit discovered that many of those for whom prayers were said demonstrated a greater medical improvement than those who were not prayed for. (Source: BBC News Online, 1999) However, another study of 800 similar patients could not detect any significant improvement between those who were prayed for and those who were not. (Source: The Times Online, 2006)

1 *Some Christians say that this sort of test is pointless because a loving God is unlikely to refuse to help people who were not lucky enough to be prayed for. What do you think?*

Going on a pilgrimage

Some Christians decide to go to a sacred place in the hope of finding a cure for their illness. There are many holy places that attract pilgrims. Lourdes, in the south of France, is the most well-known site with around 6 million people visiting it every year. That represents a lot of faith in miracles!

2 *Use the Internet to discover what happened at Lourdes in 1852 which has drawn people there in the hope of a miracle cure. Present your findings as a magazine article.*

What happens at Lourdes today?

People with illnesses visit Lourdes to bathe in the waters, which come from an underground spring and are channelled into proper bathhouses. Here, the sick are supervised by nurses and helpers. Some prefer to walk, or be pushed in their wheelchair, around the different parts of the site so that they can pray quietly or take part in services.

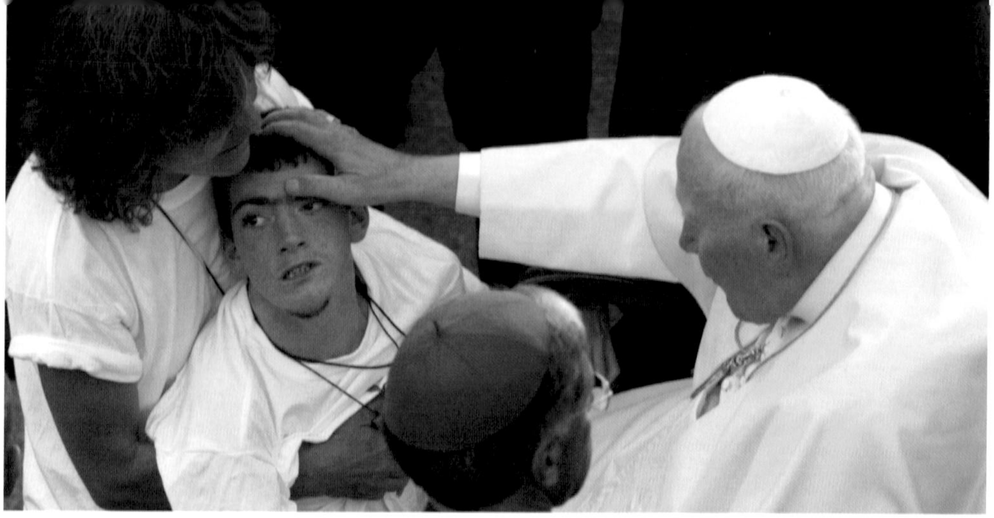

Pope John Paul II blessing a sick young man at Lourdes.

There are, however, many more people who come as pilgrims and do not suffer from any illness. They just want to absorb the atmosphere of this sacred place because they believe it will bring them closer to God.

Do miracles happen there?

There are people who believe they have been cured as a result of visiting Lourdes. The Catholic Church studies all claims carefully before confirming them as miracles, as you will discover on page 75. Of the 7000 miracle healings that have been claimed, only 66 have ever been authenticated. What many Christians find is that the healing they receive is not bodily. After going there feeling scared, angry or confused about their illness, they return from Lourdes feeling more peaceful and better able to deal with it.

3 *Write a postcard from a modern pilgrim visiting Lourdes.*

4 *Some Christians believe that healing miracles are possible but that they may not happen in the way people expect. Can you explain what people might expect from a miracle and then say what might actually happen.*

A tiny miracle

Deep in the heart of Wales is the small church of St Melangell, which was a pilgrimage site in medieval times. Christians came to touch the saint's bones in the hope they would be cured from their illness. Today, The St Melangell Centre has developed close by. It helps people with emotional, spiritual and mental health needs to find healing.

This tiny church in Wales has been a site of pilgrimage since medieval times.

5 *What would you say to those who want pilgrimage sites closed down because there is no proof that people are healed and they believe the sites only raise false hopes?*

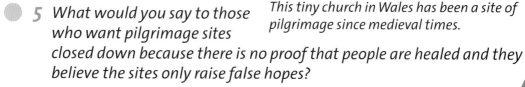

4.5 Case study of a miraculous cure

Let's examine, in detail, the case of Jean-Pierre Bely, whose recovery from a terrible illness in 1999 was so amazing that the Catholic Church declared it an official miracle.

The patient

Name: Jean-Pierre Bely

Profession: Hospital nurse in France

Year of birth: 1936

Date illness began: 1971

Symptoms:
At first, there were only slight problems such as tiredness, lack of suppleness and mobility in hands, and pins and needles in his fingertips. Gradually these symptoms got worse.

Official diagnosis:
In 1984 his illness was diagnosed as multiple sclerosis, after a severe attack left Mr Bely partly paralysed. He was diagnosed from blood tests and a lumbar puncture.

Other relevant information:
By 1987, Mr Bely was so disabled that he was bedridden and began receiving a full invalidity pension. His house was adapted to cope with his severe disability.

Visit to Lourdes:
Autumn of 1987.

His account of the first part of the experience during Mass at Lourdes:
At that moment, everything was turned upside down and I was sucked into a whirlwind of emotion – of joy, of peace and an extraordinary feeling of serenity that came over me which remains with me still, to this day. (Speaking on BBC Radio 4, 11 January 2002.)

1

His account of the second part of the healing experience later the same day:
I was lying in the sickroom, lying on the bed and felt terribly cold like an intense chill in my bones. But slowly it got warmer and warmer until it felt like a fire burning through the whole of my body. I was overwhelmed by it. I heard this voice, like an order, 'Get up and walk!' And then, all of a sudden, I don't know how, I found myself sitting up on the bed – my legs dangling over the edge and I started to touch the back of my hands. I realised I had regained mobility and sensitivity in my spine and shoulders which had been blocked for years. They were normal. In fact you could say that I'd found normality again. (Speaking on BBC Radio 4, 11 January 2002.)

The next stage:
Mr Bely was able to walk and returned home without any signs of his former illness. They have never reoccurred.

The official medical investigation:
All Mr Bely's medical records were sent from his home town to the medical bureau at Lourdes, along with a letter from him and another from his GP explaining all the stages of his illness. These were examined in detail.

Mr Bely was then called to Lourdes to be examined by various groups of doctors. The process lasted 11 years and he was examined by many, many doctors; sometimes as many as 100 during a visit. He also underwent extensive medical checks including brain scans.

The medical verdict:
In 1999, medical tests were completed. Mr Bely's cure was officially stated to be 'medically inexplicable' and the case was passed to the International Medical Committee of Lourdes.

The final verdict on a miracle:
In February 1999, Jean-Pierre Bely's recovery from multiple sclerosis was officially declared a miracle.

2

1 *What two questions would you like to email to Mr Bely?*

2 *Role-play a discussion between a Christian and an atheist on the subject of Mr Bely's cure.*

3 *Write a magazine article about this case. You are free to include your own theories about what happened.*

Miracles in other religions

Miracles are not restricted to Christianity. Here we look at Jewish, Muslim and Hindu attitudes to miracles.

There are stories of miraculous happenings in most world religions but they do not hold such a central role as they do in Christianity.

Islam

Muslims have no doubt that miracles can happen but they are not of major importance in Islam. The Qur'an and other holy writings refer to accounts of miracles associated with the Prophet Muhammad. On one occasion, Muhammad and a companion were being chased by a hostile army so they hid in a cave. A spider spun its web across the entrance and fooled Muhammad's pursuers into thinking that the cave had been empty for a long time. Another account relates to the time when Muhammad was asleep and he was taken by the Angel Gabriel on a journey to Jerusalem and up to the heavens where he met the prophets. Some of the healing miracles of Jesus, who is a prophet in Islam (see pages 110–111), are also recorded in the Qur'an.

The way the Qur'an was given to humanity and the fact that it has survived unchanged for centuries is the greatest miracle in Islam.

Muslims accept that miracles can happen and, in earlier times, miracles often convinced people that a man was indeed a prophet. But by far the most important miracle is the Qur'an. The way God gave the book to humanity is seen as a miracle (see page 63) and the way God's words have remained unchanged ever since also seems miraculous.

Judaism

There are many stories in the Hebrew Bible (which Christians call the Old Testament) containing miraculous occurrences (see page 68). Most Jews think that these events did happen but it is not essential to believe in them. They believe that what really matters is the message behind the stories. The story of Moses and his followers crossing the Red Sea teaches Jews to trust in God when faced with danger. It is said that reports of miracles are supposed to inspire and teach people in a way that factual events don't. In Judaism, the important miracles can be seen in the natural world around us.

1 *Draw a poster, or diagram, to show the different ways that two religions regard miracles.*

Hinduism

Hindus also believe that miraculous events can take place. In 1995 there were reports of a statue of the god Ganesh drinking milk that had been offered on a spoon by a worshipper. The story travelled fast and teaspoons of milk were offered to statues around the world with the same effect. Scientists believe that this could be explained as an example of capillary action. Many statues are hollow or filled with absorbent material that could have soaked up the milk. But the reason for this apparent phenomenon was less important than the effect. The miracle of the milk brought many Hindus to worship at the temple, reminded others of their religious duties and convinced others of the existence of God – that was the miracle.

These children offered milk on a spoon to a small statue of Ganesh. The milk disappeared from the spoon.

2 *Role-play, or write, an interview between someone who has witnessed a miracle and someone who believes they have a natural explanation for the event.*

3 *'Miracles don't do any good to anybody.' What would you say to that?*

Picture this!

In September 1918, Padre Pio, a Catholic priest (who died in 1968), suffered wounds on his hands and head in exactly the same places as those Jesus received on the cross. Such wounds apparently ooze blood continuously and cause a lot of discomfort. They are called stigmata and are said to appear miraculously on a holy man who is permitted to know something of the pain that Jesus suffered. This is a very controversial form of miracle, which dates back to St Francis of Assisi in the Middle Ages. Many fakes have been exposed over the years but most Catholics are convinced that Padre Pio's stigmata were genuine.

1 *Why do you think this picture is included in a unit of work on miracles?*

Just to recap

All through this unit of work we have been looking at the sort of things people regard as miracles. We have also considered different approaches towards miraculous events and what they mean for believers.

Let's remind ourselves of what we have learned:

We began by thinking about what people mean when they talk about miracles. **A** How would you define a miracle? **B** Why is a miracle different from a magic trick?	**We looked** at the Christian view of miracles and those performed by Jesus. **A** What do Christians think is the purpose of miracles? **B** Name one sort of miracle performed by Jesus?
We considered medical miracles and examined one case closely. **A** Name one pilgrimage site where medical miracles are believed to have happened. **B** What could people gain besides healing from a visit there?	**We went on to look** at the views of Islam, Judaism and Hinduism on miracles. **A** What would Muslims claim was the greatest miracle in their religion? **B** How do Jews regard miracles?

We started by thinking about miraculous events in the past. Now that you have completed this unit of work, do you think there is such a thing as a miracle today?

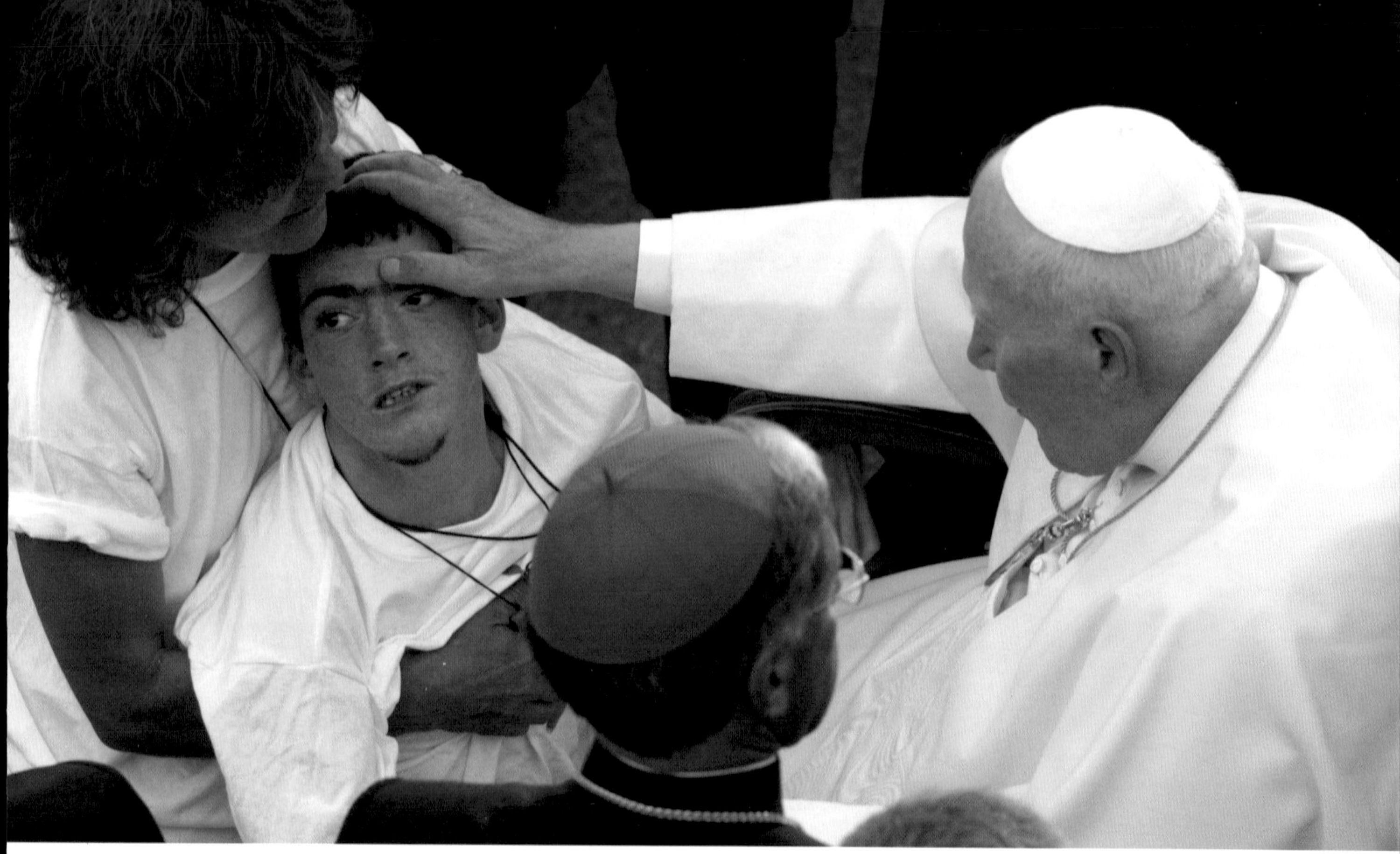

Some people say that it is unkind to mention the idea of miracle cures to people who are sick. Do you agree? Should places such as Lourdes (shown above) be banned because they create false hopes or do you think they can do some good?

Choose one of the following tasks to check your progress in this unit.

Task one

a *What sort of events would a Muslim or Jew class as miraculous?*

b *Explain how Christians would distinguish a miracle from a coincidence or a magic trick.*

c *'People who claim that they have been miraculously cured are just deluding themselves.' What do you think about this statement? What might someone who disagrees with you say?*

Task two

a *What is meant by the term 'a miracle cure'?*

b *Explain why Christians think Jesus carried out miracles.*

c *'There is no such thing as a miracle.' What do you think about this statement? What would people who disagree with you say?*

4.9 Something extra

1 *The following was Scottish philosopher David Hume's opinion of miracles:*

'Miracles go against the laws of nature. The laws of nature are based on the common experience of millions of people. What a few witnesses to a miracle claim to have seen, when weighed against the common experience of millions of people, must mean it is more likely that the few witnesses got it wrong.'

a *Does David Hume believe in miracles or not?*

b *Re-write Hume's case more simply so a ten year old could understand it. You can use an example if you wish.*

c *Do you think he is right or wrong? Why?*

In 2007, Madeleine McCann was snatched from her bed during a family holiday in Portugal. Her parents, who are Roman Catholic, visited the shrine at Fatima, pictured above, to pray for a miracle in the search for their daughter.

2 *Find out what happened at Fatima in 1917 that has made it such an important holy site today. What miracles are recorded to have taken place as a result of pilgrimages to Fatima? Use your research to create a folded A4 leaflet about this pilgrimage site.*

3 *Script a radio interview between Diane, the presenter of 'Faith Today', who is a sceptic but wants to give listeners a fair impression of the subject, and Peter Fansom, who believes he has experienced a miracle.*

4

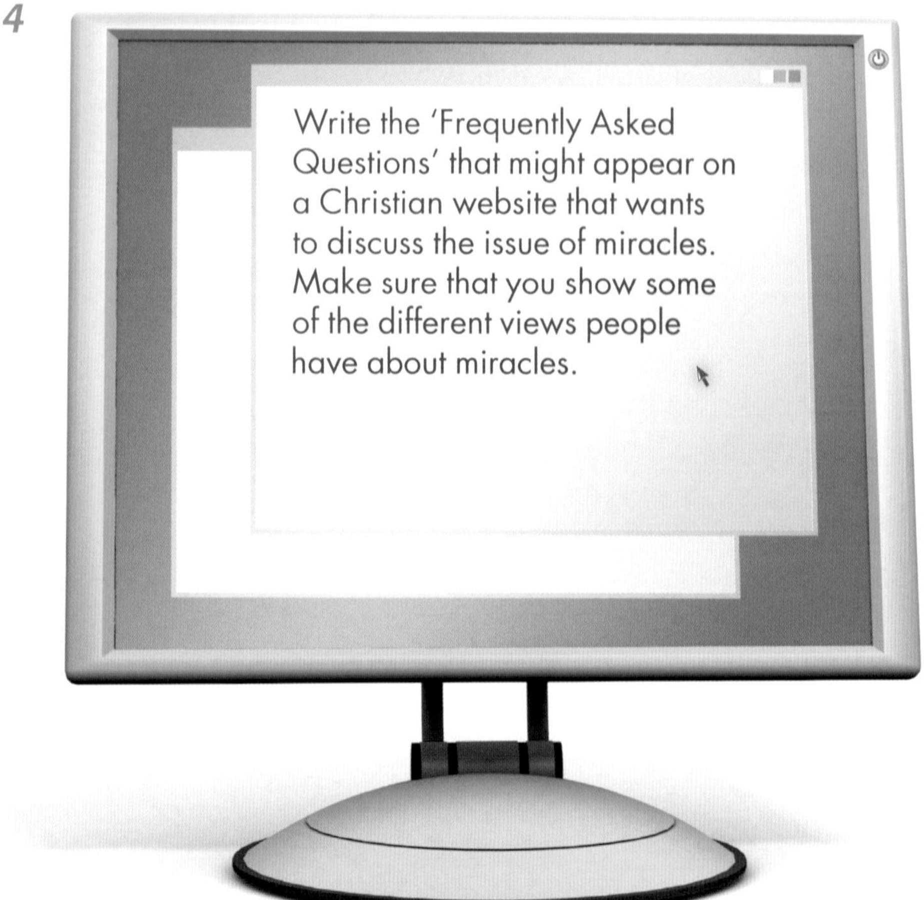
Write the 'Frequently Asked Questions' that might appear on a Christian website that wants to discuss the issue of miracles. Make sure that you show some of the different views people have about miracles.

5 *Some people say there is no such thing as a miracle and that everything has a cause. Would you agree?*

6 *Make a poster about some of the different miracles Jesus performed. You can offer natural explanations for what happened if you wish. Alongside each, add what Christians believe such miracles are saying about the nature of Jesus.*

7 *How would you reply to Jake's letter (below)?*

'My mum is ill and we don't know what is wrong with her. Do you think it would make any difference if I prayed for her? I am not a Christian and don't really believe in God.'

UNIT 5

Science rules OK!

In this unit we consider whether science and religion are really sworn enemies. We also investigate the different approaches each has to understanding the origins of life on earth.

5.1 Consider the difference between scientific knowledge and other forms of knowledge.

5.2 Examine the way believers arrive at knowledge.

5.3 Look at the different approaches to the origin of the universe.

5.4 Examine the clash that exists over the origin of humans.

5.5 Study the attitudes of three eminent scientists to the debate.

5.6 Investigate the contribution that science has made.

Science rules OK!

5.1 How do we know?

Let's examine what we understand by scientific knowledge and consider the ways of knowing something.

It's all questions

We all ask questions from an early age. You have only got to think of the three year old who begins, 'What's that?' You tell him it's a man crossing the road. 'Why is he crossing the road?' the boy asks. You reply, 'To go to the shop', only to be asked, 'Why is he going to the shop?' And so it goes on. Whatever answer you give produces another question.

What the child is trying to do is to make sense of the world around him. It's something we do all our lives and is also one of the things that distinguishes us from animals. It seems unlikely that a cat will reflect on what life was like last century or what might happen after she dies.

We try to make sense of our world; so does science and so does religion. In this, science and religion are in agreement!

Prove it!

The brilliant thing about scientific knowledge is that it is totally impartial. No matter who does the experiment shown in the photograph below, the outcome should be the same. That's marvellous because you know exactly where you stand. The strange thing is that scientists don't often claim to have totally proved something. They usually say that they have arrived at a working hypothesis, which will be accepted as correct until it is disproved.

Let's consider their method. First the scientist asks: 'Why is this happening?' Then they decide on a hypothesis that is a possible explanation for what they are investigating. To see if their hypothesis is true, lots of identical experiments will be carried out. If the outcome is the same, the hypothesis is accepted until new evidence disproves it.

This is only one of many tests that a scientist will carry out using exactly the same method to prove that the results are reliable.

1. *Make up three questions that can only be answered by a scientific method.*
2. *Make up three questions that can't be answered scientifically.*

Can't prove it!

People often assume that a scientific method is the best way of finding an answer but in reality we use lots of ways. Some things are impossible to prove scientifically.

3 *What methods do you use to prove that:*

- *brussel sprouts (or fill in your own pet dislike) taste horrible?*
- *you are in love?*
- *ghosts and fairies do (or don't) exist?*
- *the Battle of Hastings took place in 1066?*

Prove it beyond reasonable doubt

That is what a jury is asked to do, as it is extremely difficult to prove something scientifically in a court of law. Evidence is presented to 12 ordinary people and they have to decide, and agree, on what really happened.

When you study this optical illusion, do you see the beautiful young woman or the old hag? Could science and religion ever look at the same thing and see something different? Perhaps neither of their conclusions is wrong – they are just different.

4 *Design a poster to show different ways of discovering the truth.*

And finally

It is worth remembering what the author Oscar Wilde famously wrote in *The Importance of Being Earnest*: 'The truth is rarely pure and never simple.'

5.2 Is religious knowledge something different?

Here we examine what it is that makes religious knowledge different from scientific or any other form of knowledge.

People arrive at their religious knowledge and beliefs in various ways. Some are shown here. Not everyone will use all four ways to arrive at their knowledge and it is likely that they will rate some as more important than others. It is also possible that they may reject some of these forms totally.

Personal experience

What can convince people that there is a God who takes an active part in the life of humans is something that happens to them personally. We examined miracles in Unit 4 and they are certainly a powerful experience, but only a few people experience miracles. It is more likely that someone would believe they have felt God's presence, not in any dramatic way but as quiet support when they needed it. This certainly can never be proved but, again, what really matters is not what happened but how the person interprets their experience.

Books

The importance that believers place on books varies. For a Muslim, the Qur'an is without doubt the word of God and everything in it is true and not open to doubt. Some Christians have the same belief about the Bible and accept all passages at face value – you have probably heard the phrase 'gospel truth'. As we learned in *REflections 1* (Unit 6), Christians have a variety of approaches to the Bible. Many believe that the Bible contains words inspired by God, written by humans and then passed down the generations. This means errors and misunderstandings may have crept in. Nevertheless, Christians still rank the Bible above ordinary books in importance.

Faith

This is this area where you will see the biggest distinction between religion and science. Members of all religions hold opinions and knowledge as a result of faith. This means they believe and trust that what they are taught is true because it comes from God. There is no reason why God has to be answerable to man-made laws or earthly restrictions any more than life in outer space does.

RELIGIOUS KNOWLEDGE

Teachings

This is an area where science and religion might overlap. If you think about it, most people's scientific knowledge has been taught to them. No one learns it all from conducting experiments. Any knowledge may have been passed directly from a teacher or transmitted from a book. It may be accepted as accurate information because the source is considered trustworthy and reliable. Religion is just the same. A religious teacher or a book could be the authority that passes the information on. In both religion and science, students have to accept the information on trust because they aren't in a position to check every single point for themselves.

1. *Draw a similar spider diagram to the one above showing four possible sources of either historical knowledge or geographical knowledge.*
2. *How would you rank the importance of the four major sources of religious knowledge? Decide how you would rank the importance of the sources for the subject you worked on in question 1.*
3. *What do you think are the weaknesses in each of the four areas displayed on this and the previous page?*

5.3 God or the Big Bang?

Current scientific thinking states that our universe began as the result of a cosmic explosion. So where does that leave God?

Here we look at the different views about the creation of the universe and decide whether they are totally at odds with one another.

The origin of the universe is a key area where science and religion can come into conflict. Because scientists constantly develop different hypotheses and test them, as we discovered on page 86, there are regular changes and new ideas in their understanding of things. The origin of the universe is one such area, as scientist Michael Poole explains:

According to current thinking, there was a Big Bang some 13 billion years ago. This was not a gigantic explosion in black, empty space at some point in time, because space and time did not exist; they came into being at the Big Bang...

As a result of the Big Bang, matter moved apart at nearly the speed of light [186,000 miles a second]. But gravity tried to pull it together again. According to Professor Paul Davies, if the explosion had differed in strength at the outset by only one part in 10 (to the power 60), the universe we now perceive would not exist...

As the universe expanded, gravity brought clusters of matter together to form stars.

Stars are gigantic nuclear furnaces like monster hydrogen bombs. In them, the lightest elements (hydrogen and helium) are 'cooked up' into heavier ones like carbon, nitrogen and oxygen, the building blocks of life. This takes thousands of millions of years, since gravity is a weak force. Stars of a certain size finally blow up, scattering these elements into space.

Our bodies are formed from the ashes of long-dead stars. We are made of stardust.

(Source: 'RE Today' Summer 1998)

1 *Write the 'Frequently Asked Questions' page for a website about the Big Bang.*

Try to write three questions and answers. Use page 90 to help you. You can research further information to add to it.

The Bible says:

'In the beginning, when God created the universe, the earth was formless and desolate. The raging ocean that covered everything was engulfed in total darkness, and the power of God was moving over the water. Then God commanded, "Let there be light" – and light appeared.'

(Genesis 1:1–3)

The big clash!

Creation is the area where most people think religion and science clash. The author of the scientific account on the left-hand page, Michael Poole, is both a scientist and a Christian. As you will have noticed, he has no problem accepting the Big Bang theory. This is because he believes that science tells us *how* the universe began, whereas the Bible tells us *why* the universe began. For some Christians, the account of God creating the world in six days, which appears in Genesis, is like a fable. It was told to explain to people that the universe was deliberately created by God and not simply an accident or the result of some random activity. They would argue that the Big Bang was the method God used to bring the universe into being.

Those Christians who disagree with this view are convinced that the Bible gives us an accurate, factual account of the way God created the world in six days. These Christians, often called 'Creationists', point out that the Bible is the word of God, but the Big Bang is only a theory. Scientists have not got any absolute proof that creation really happened that way.

2 *There is an ongoing Internet debate between the Creationists, who believe the world was created by God as it says in the Bible, and other Christians, who believe in the Big Bang theory.*

- *Write brief entries from four different people who want to make their views known and want to comment on what the person before them wrote.*

3 *'The Big Bang theory proves there isn't a God.' What would you say to this statement?*

Man or monkey?

Here we examine some of the ideas people have about the origins of human life.

According to the Natural History Museum, monkeys and humans share 99.4 per cent of the same DNA.

'Then God commanded: "Let the earth produce all kinds of animal life: domestic and wild, large and small" – and it was done.... Then God said, "And now we will make human beings; they will be like us and resemble us. They will have power over the fish, the birds, and all animals, domestic and wild, large and small." So God created human beings, making them to be like himself. He created them male and female.'

(Genesis 1:24–28)

1 *Explain why there might be a problem accepting the extract from the book of Genesis, above, and the fact that we share 99.4 per cent of the same DNA as monkeys.*

Any problem?

You may have noticed, in Genesis Chapter 1, it says that God made humans distinctly separate from other animals. It also says that human beings were made like God. This could mean many things, such as humans have the same appearance, although this seems unlikely. Some believers interpret this to mean that we have the powers of reasoning and intelligence that enable us to grow closer to God.

Evolution

In the 1850s, Charles Darwin came up with a different theory about the origins of life on earth. His 'Theory of Evolution' said that all animals have developed as a result of 'Natural Selection'. He said that the animals best suited to their environment survive, breed and pass on their genes to the next generation. The rest die out or are eaten.

That all sounds a bit cruel, and a long way from the idea of a loving God who put each particular species on earth and then created humans quite separately from the rest of the animal kingdom. There is, however, fossil evidence to support Darwin's theory.

2 *Use the Natural History Museum's website, found at www.nhm.ac.uk/, to find out current ideas on evolution. Report your findings as a newspaper article.*

This reconstruction is from an adult skeleton, only one metre tall, that was found in an Indonesian cave in 2004. Scientists nicknamed him 'The Hobbit'. Could this be an early human?

Does Darwin win?

Well, not exactly. While there is evidence of the evolution of certain animals, there is no definite proof that humans are descended from apes. As humans, we are distinctly different from the rest of the animal kingdom in several ways. For example, we are the only animals that can use tools to make tools. Admittedly, birds and monkeys do select objects to use as tools but they don't actually make them. Then there is the question of our sense of humour, power of speech, appreciation of beauty and romantic love. It could be argued that no other animals display signs of these. Any answers?

In the 150 years since Darwin suggested the link between man and ape, many early skeletons have been unearthed. There is now lots of scientific evidence to show that we are *related* to apes, but none, so far, to show that we are *descended* from apes.

Where does that leave us?

3 *Write three entries for a natural history website about the evolution of humans, giving the views of:*

a a person who takes the Bible literally;

b a person who is convinced that Darwin's Theory of Evolution can explain the origins of man;

c someone who is unsure.

Meet the scientists

Here, some eminent scientists discuss why they see no conflict between their work and their beliefs.

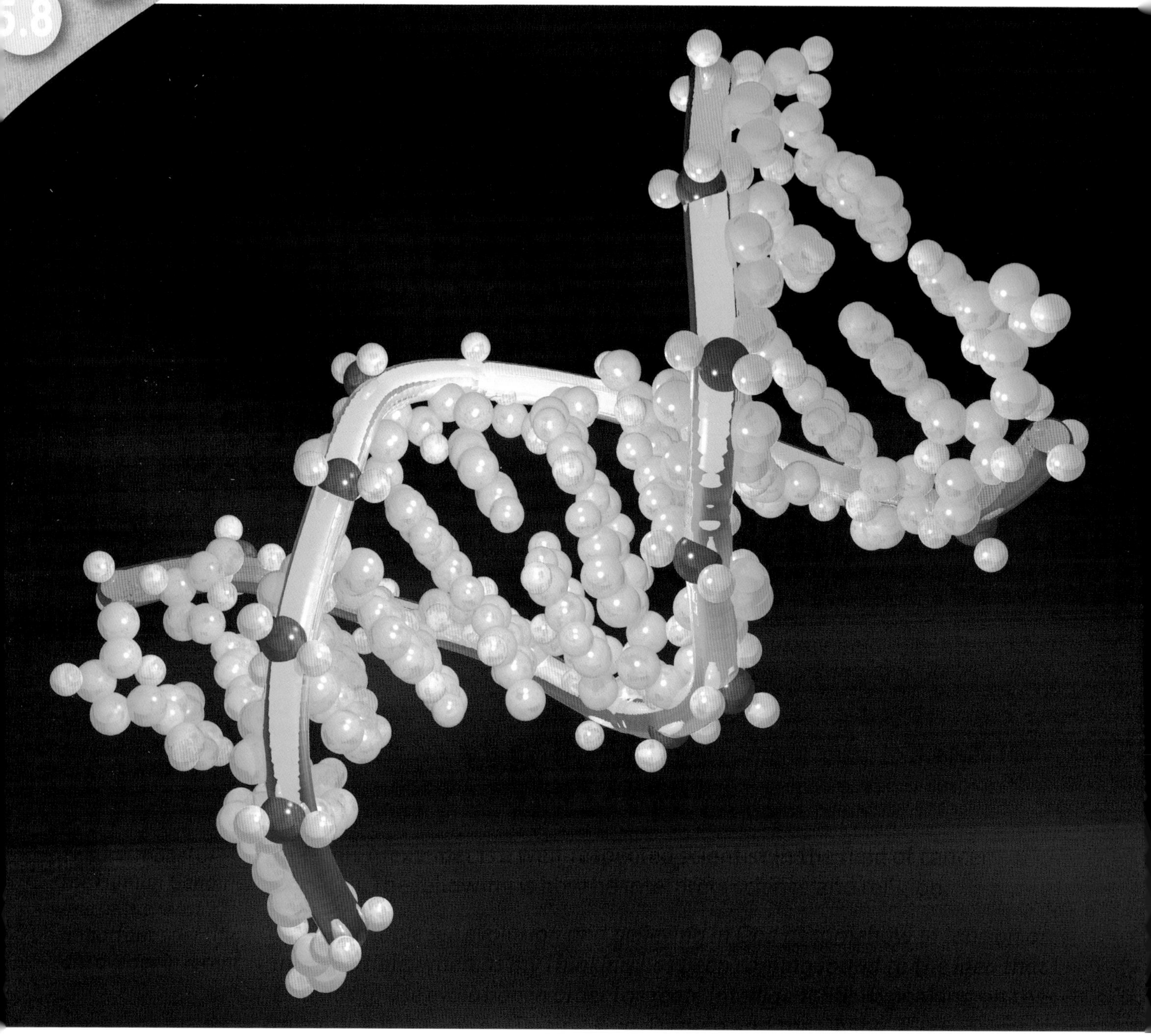

This is a model of the Human Genome, one of the most important scientific discoveries in recent years.

Dr Denis Alexander is a well-respected scientist in the field of cancer research. The following is how he interprets science and religion:

'A lot of people see evolution and believing in God as somehow in tension or incompatible, whereas my thinking has been coming round to the idea that God has to use evolution in order to create intelligent life.' (Speaking on the television programme 'Testing God: Darwin and the Divine'.)

Professor Jocelyn Bell Burnell is a highly respected astronomer and a Quaker. She was part of the team that discovered pulsars or collapsed stars. Here are her thoughts about creation:

'From what I have learnt as an astronomer I believe that the universe evolved itself without any active participation from God, and it seems reasonable to me that the world continues, at least on a grand scale, to evolve by itself – that God does not directly interfere with the running of the world; but that he does through people and their attitudes....' (Source: Philadelphia Yearly Meeting of the Religious Society of Friends, 1976)

The Rev. Dr John Polkinghorne was Cambridge professor of mathematical physics before becoming a priest. He was asked whether science had disproved religion.

'It would seem to me that it couldn't be so. I believe that science is asking one set of questions about the world – the 'how' questions and religion is asking the 'why' questions. These questions do not contradict each other. We can ask and answer both questions about the same thing. If I raise my hand it is because it is my willed intention, perhaps to give you a cheerful wave. On the other hand we can have a description of how the muscles of my body work. These two descriptions are not at odds with each other, they are complementary descriptions of the same reality. In the same way I think that science and religion are complementary descriptions of the very rich and varied world of our experience.' (Source: RE Today 863, 1991)

1 *Choose one of the three scientists mentioned here and explain why they do not see any problem in being both a Christian and a scientist.*

2 *Explain what Dr Polkinghorne is saying when he compares religion and science with putting his hand in the air?*

The following is the Humanist view of evolution. Humanists do not believe there is sufficient evidence to prove that God exists.

Millions of years of evolution by natural selection (which continues even now) happened to produce Homo sapiens, human beings, one species amongst the many and various species that exist and have existed. And you are one individual of our species, here because your parents conceived you. No other reason. It is a wonder that you exist, and your uniqueness is amazing! We should also celebrate how much humans have managed to find out about how we got here – we are a remarkable species. (British Humanist Association)

3 *How do Humanists give meaning to our existence without needing to involve God?*

5.6 Islam and science

Let's examine the long association Muslims have had with scientific discoveries.

> *'An hour's study of nature is better than a year's prayer.'*
>
> (Muhammad)

From this quotation, you can see that Muslims have no problem with scientific investigation. What Muhammad was saying was that a detailed study of God's creation will lead people closer to God. This is supported by various passages in the Qur'an, where believers are urged to discover the truth about the world and to question things, so that they can arrive at the truth. This seems to support scientific methods of investigation.

Muslims have always valued the use of human intellect because it is a gift from God. Unlike the problems scientists such as Galileo faced with the Catholic Church, Muslims have never regarded science and religion as separate areas. The Golden Age of Islamic science was in the early medieval period when Christian Europe was going through a dark time in terms of science. As you will see, the developments of modern science owe a great debt to these early Islamic scholars. The following are a few fields where Islamic scholars particularly shone.

Astronomy

Because the Islamic calendar is a lunar one (the one used in the Western world is a solar calendar), a good knowledge of astronomy was essential for calculating when the months begin and end, especially the holy month of Ramadan when fasting takes place. Muslim studies went far beyond that. Scholars found out exactly what caused a rainbow. The studies of astronomer Abu al-Fida have led to his name being given to a crater on the moon.

Muslim astronomers were far ahead of the rest of the world in their observations and understanding of the moon.

Mathematics

Today we use Arabic numbers, whereas in earlier times Roman numerals were used. You have only got to try working out a simple calculation such as 'CXII + LVIII' to realise the difficulties of advancing the study of maths very far. There is another difficulty with Roman numerals – there is no symbol for a zero. If you think about it for a while, you will realise how limiting that is for some calculations. We have Muslim mathematicians to thank for zero. They also retrieved the work of ancient Greek scholars, such as Euclid, translated their work into Arabic and then built on it. We also have Muslim scholars to thank for the decimal system.

1 *Muslim scholars were responsible for developing 'al-jabr'. What particular part of maths is that? (Hint: pronounce it!)*

Medicine

Hospitals appeared in major Islamic towns and their organisation was impressive. Patients suffering from fevers were separated from the rest because Muslim doctors were aware of contagious diseases. They studied smallpox to discover its origin and in the process came to understand something about how the immune system worked. Ibn Zuhr, a twelfth-century physician, perfected surgical and post-mortem techniques. The search for cures led some to study botany and the production of an encyclopaedia of medicinal plants.

2 *Explain why Islam does not think religion and science are in conflict .*

ZOOM LENS 17-55mm 1:2.8
ø77mm
LENS MADE IN JAPAN

The original ideas for both these optical devices came from Ibn al-Haytham, a first-century Egyptian who studied the functions of the eye and the behaviour of light.

3 *Write an entry for a science website giving some idea of the contribution Islam has made to scientific development.*

To finish

It has been said that, without the contribution of early Muslim scholars, modern science would have taken a lot longer to develop.

Picture this!

The Milky Way is estimated to contain over 100 billion stars. What is the quotation below, from the book of Psalms, saying about the Milky Way?

'How clearly the sky reveals God's glory!

How plainly it shows what he has done!'

(Psalms 19:1)

Islamic scholars were some of the first astronomers. What connections are there between Islam and the night sky?

5.8 Just to recap

In this unit of work we have been considering whether religion and science are sworn enemies. We looked in detail at areas such as creation and evolution, and considered the contribution Islam has made to scientific knowledge.

Let's remind ourselves of what we have learned:

We began by looking at the different types of ways that we know things. **A** How does a court of law distinguish what the truth is? **B** How do scientists arrive at the truth?	**We went on to look** at different views about the Big Bang and evolution. **A** How does Darwin explain the origin of human beings? **B** Why do some Christians reject his theory?
We studied the opinions of some scientists who hold religious beliefs. **A** How can people believe in God and the Big Bang? **B** What do the 'how' and 'why' questions of science and religion refer to?	**We examined in detail** the contribution that Islam has made to science. **A** Why do Muslims encourage scientific study? **B** Name one scientific development that a Muslim was responsible for.

We started with the idea that religion and science could not exist together. Now that you have completed this unit, would it be correct to say that they are sworn enemies?

What possible explanations are there for the beginning of the world? Which do you think is the most likely and why?

Choose one of the following tasks to check your progress in this unit.

Task one

a *What does the Bible say about the creation of humans?*

b *Explain two different opinions that Christians might have about the meaning of the Genesis story of creation.*

c *'Science has destroyed religion.' What do you think about this statement? What would someone who disagreed with you say?*

Task two

a *Why does Islam encourage the study of science?*

b *Explain how religious knowledge can be different from scientific knowledge.*

c *'God or the Big Bang – a Christian can't believe in both.' What would you say about this statement? What might someone who disagrees with you say?*

5.9 Something extra

1 *Design a poster, entitled 'Man or Monkey?', showing the two sides of this argument. What is your own view on evolution?*

2 *The conflict between science and religion began in the medieval period. One of the most serious clashes was between the scientist Galileo and the Roman Catholic Church. Find out what it was that they could not agree on and what happened to Galileo. Give a presentation to the class about this clash.*

3 *Richard Dawkins, a leading professor in evolutionary biology and also an atheist, is a well-known critic of religion. Here are some of his comments on the religion and science debate. Choose one of his attacks on religion and explain the point he is making. Then give your own views on his comments.*

- *'I am against religion because it teaches us to be satisfied with not understanding the world.'*
- *'It is grindingly, creakingly, crashingly obvious that if Darwinism was really a theory of chance, it could not work.'*
- *'Religious people split into three main groups when faced with science. I shall label them the "know-nothings", the "know-alls", and the "no-contests".'*
- *'Most people, I believe, think that you need a God to explain the existence of the world, and especially the existence of life. They are wrong, but our education system is such that many people don't know it.'*
- *'Religions do make claims about the universe – the same kinds of claims that scientists make, except they're usually false.'*

Professor Richard Dawkins is a leading evolutionary scientist and an outspoken critic of religion.

4

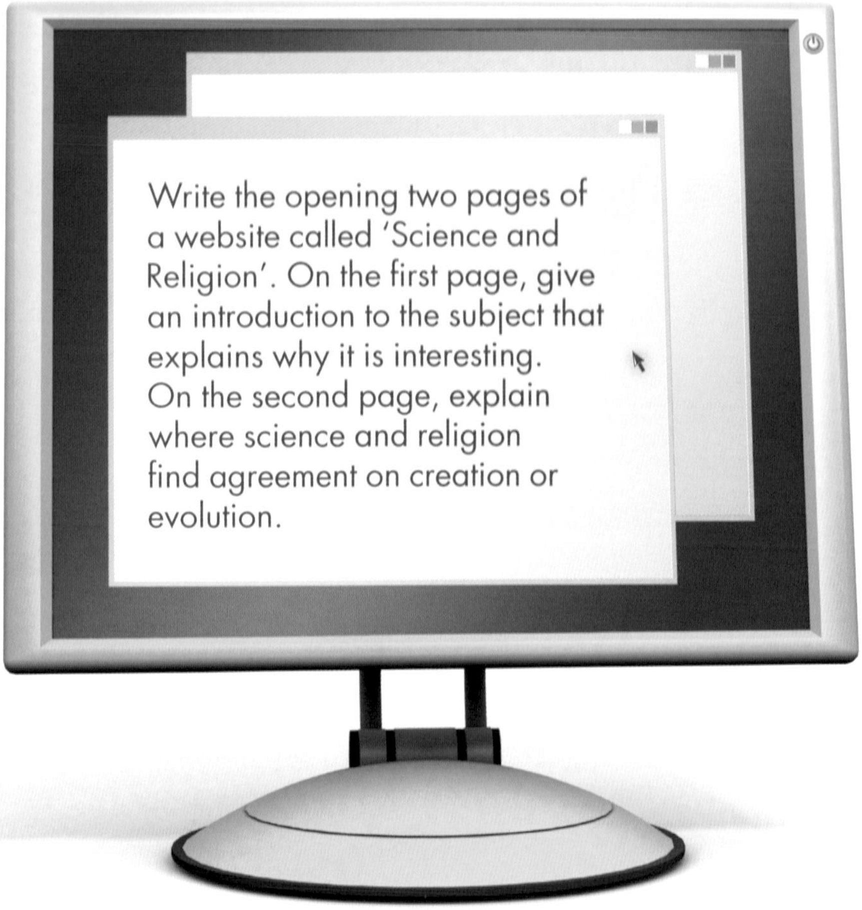
Write the opening two pages of a website called 'Science and Religion'. On the first page, give an introduction to the subject that explains why it is interesting. On the second page, explain where science and religion find agreement on creation or evolution.

5 *Construct an acrostic poem about EVOLUTION. See if you can show two sides of this debate.*

6 *The great Albert Einstein once said: 'Science without religion is lame, religion without science is blind.' This was his version of the argument that religion and science are both trying to understand the world in different ways. Give your own views about whether you think it is possible to be a scientist and hold religious beliefs.*

7 *In Alabama, USA, biology textbooks today must carry a warning on the front, similar to that shown on the book on the right. As a class, discuss whether you think this should also appear on textbooks in the UK to give us a fair balance in the evolution debate.*

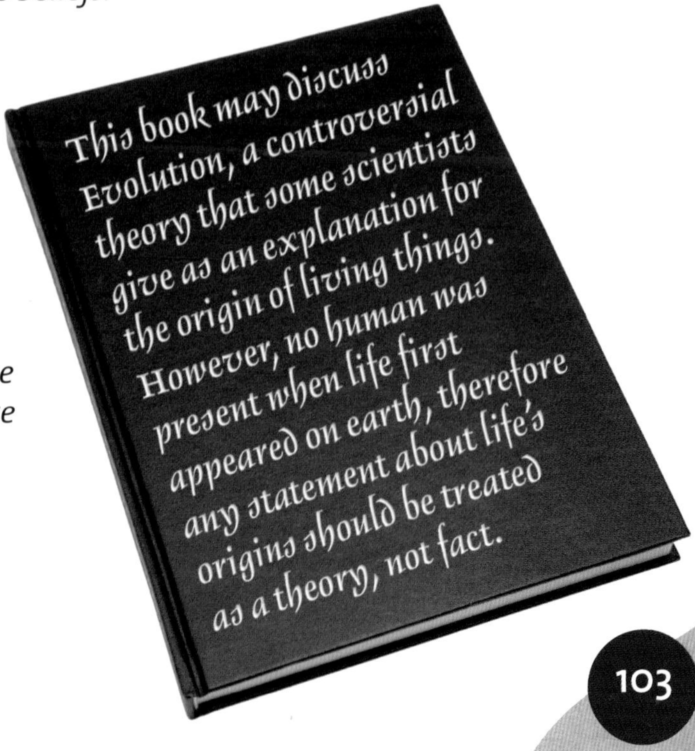
This book may discuss Evolution, a controversial theory that some scientists give as an explanation for the origin of living things. However, no human was present when life first appeared on earth, therefore any statement about life's origins should be treated as a theory, not fact.

UNIT

6 Someone special?

Jesus is one of the most famous names on the planet. In this unit we examine why that is the case and what is actually known about him.

6.1 Investigate the extraordinary appeal of Jesus approximately 2000 years later.

6.2 Examine the historical evidence to support Jesus' existence.

6.3 Consider the Muslim view of Jesus.

6.4 Investigate the Christian view of Jesus as divine.

6.5 Look at the humanity of Jesus and his teachings.

6.6 Investigate why some people think Jesus' teachings are revolutionary.

Someone special?

6.1 Why the big interest?

Let's investigate how much interest there is in Jesus and some of the different responses to this man's life.

Biggest name in history

For someone who lived in a tiny country and has been dead for almost 2000 years, Jesus is surprisingly well-known around the world. In fact, it is difficult to think of anybody to rival his long-standing international fame. The two pictures on these pages belong to unexpected twenty-first century 'hits' that centred on the life of Jesus.

The Number One New York Times Bestseller
DAN BROWN
THE DA VINCI CODE
'Fascinating and absorbing ... A great, riveting read. I loved this book' HARLAN COBEN

Used by permission of The Random House Group Ltd.

In 2004, this book was an unexpected best-seller, selling more than 60 million copies in 44 languages. Its plot centres on the supposition that Jesus married Mary Magdalene and that they have descendants. This is something that the Church states is totally untrue. However, the book produced a renewed interest in Jesus' life and record numbers visited sites that the book said were connected with him.

1 *List ten people that you think could claim to be amongst the biggest names in history and rank them in order of fame. Would you include Jesus in the list? Share the list with the class to devise a list of the group's top ten most famous people ever.*

Some different responses to Jesus

JESUS

MYTH

Some people argue that Jesus never existed at all. They say that the stories handed down about him are simply fictional. The stories contain all the key ingredients you might expect in the tale of a mythical hero: a magical birth, supernatural events and victories over dark forces.

FACT

Other people point to facts in the gospel stories about Jesus that can be verified. These show there really was an historical person called Jesus. We will examine some of the facts in detail on page 109.

FAITH

Many religious believers approach the subject of Jesus in a totally different way to the other two boxes here. For them, the existence of Jesus is real because they have faith in God. They argue that facts and statistics can be produced to 'prove' anything and have nothing to do with belief.

2 *Discuss the following statement: 'Jesus must exist because fairy-tale heroes like Jack the giant killer and Aladdin have never had such a following.' What do you think about this opinion?*

How big is the interest?

FACT-FILE

- *2 billion people today follow Jesus' teachings*
- *30 per cent of the world's population believe in Jesus*
- *41 million British people say they are Christian*
- *Christianity is the largest religion in the world*

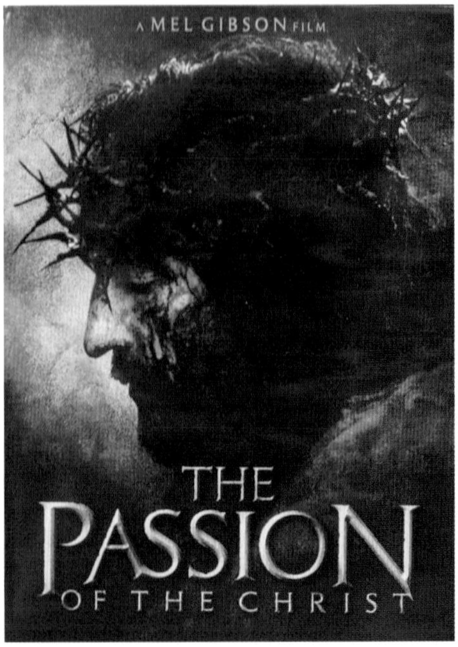
A MEL GIBSON FILM
THE PASSION OF THE CHRIST

This film was a huge box office success when it was launched in the USA in 2004. It is currently the 11th highest earning film in history, which may be surprising for a film about Jesus' crucifixion.

3 *Reply to a magazine letter that claims: 'There must be lots of Christians in the world because so many people celebrate Christmas.'*

To finish

4 *Why do you think Jesus remains so famous over 2000 years after he died?*

Was Jesus a real person?

Let's examine the historical evidence for Jesus' existence to see how convincing it is and how much it matches believers' ideas about Jesus.

This stone, discovered in 1961, is archaeological proof that Pontius Pilate existed. His name is carved in the second line.

1 *What four pieces of information would you require to prove that a historical person really existed?*

Pictures?

Images of Egyptian pharaohs exist from as early as 1500BCE but these are exceptional cases. Generally, there is no record of what 'ordinary' people looked like until photography became possible in the nineteenth century. Pictures that do exist of Jesus don't show us what he really looked like either. They are usually painted to portray an aspect of his character that the artist wants to convey. If you look forward to pages 118 and 119 you will see three such pictures. They are different from the ones on page 105.

What did the people he knew say about him?

This is another problem area when looking for concrete evidence, because most people who knew Jesus were illiterate. This was a time when the average person couldn't read or write, the printing press hadn't been invented and few things were recorded in writing. However, it meant people were much more careful than we are at handing things on by word of mouth. For this reason, the accounts of Jesus that were written after his death are likely to be fairly accurate. Mark's Gospel was written down 40 years after Jesus' death and Matthew and Luke's Gospels were written a bit later. These can be tested for historical accuracy.

The historical Jesus

Besides the gospel accounts, there is also documented evidence of Jesus' existence in other places. The Jewish historian, Flavius Josephus, included information about Jesus in one of his books. He referred to Jesus as a teacher and a worker of wonders (miracles), who gathered a band of followers that continued to follow him even after his death.

Rock tombs such as this one in Jerusalem still exist from Jesus' time. Once the body was inside the tomb, it was sealed with a large boulder to keep wild animals out.

The Roman historian, Tacitus, mentions a Christus who started a movement in the Judaea region of Israel. Christus was apparently executed during the reign of Emperor Tiberius on the orders of Pontius Pilate but as late as 64CE still had many followers in Rome, who suffered at the hands of Emperor Nero.

2 *Why is it especially helpful to have the accounts of Josephus and Tacitus?*

3 *Use the date box below to work out when Jesus might have lived. The birth stories at the beginning of Luke's Gospel say that Jesus was born when Augustus was emperor and Herod was king. When Jesus was arrested he was taken to the house of the High Priest, Caiaphas, before being taken to Pontius Pilate. Because Jesus came from Judaea, Pilate sent him to Herod.*

Some dates

Herod the Great ruled Judaea from 37BCE–4BCE

Augustus Caesar was Roman emperor from 27BCE–14CE

Tiberius was emperor from 14–37CE

Pontius Pilate was Roman governor from 26–36CE

Herod Antipas ruled Judaea from 4BCE–39CE

Caiaphas was High Priest from 18–37CE

And finally

Some Christians are not especially concerned with proving whether Jesus was an historical person or not. For them, the important thing is simply believing that he was the Son of God.

6.3 Isa

Here we examine the importance of Isa (the Arabic name for Jesus) in Islam.

عيسى

The word above is the name 'Isa', which means 'Jesus'. It is written in Arabic calligraphy.

Islam has great respect for Jesus, who is known by the Arabic name of Isa. He is the second most important prophet in the religion – after Muhammad. When Isa's name is mentioned by a Muslim, they will often say 'Peace be upon him', immediately afterwards. This is to show respect for Isa as a holy prophet.

Is Isa the same person as Jesus?

The short answer is 'yes', although Muslim beliefs about Isa are slightly different from those held by Christians. The main difference is that Muslims believe Isa was a prophet and not the Son of God. A prophet is God's messenger and a normal human being, who will live and die like any other person. This is totally unacceptable to Christians, who regard Jesus as divine because they believe that God was his father and, because Mary was his mother, he was also human.

Isa in the Qur'an

The Qur'an has a chapter called 'Mary' and tells of Mary's fright at the visit of a holy spirit, who came in the form of a young man. He was the angel Jibril (Gabriel), the same angel who brought the words of the Qur'an to Muhammad.

'"I am your Lord's emissary," he replied, "and have come to give you a holy son."

"How shall I bear a child," she answered, "when I have neither been touched by any man nor ever been unchaste?"

"Thus did your Lord speak," he replied. "That is easy enough for Me. He shall be a sign to mankind and a blessing from Ourself. This is Our decree."

Thereupon she conceived him, and retired to a far-off place.' (19:19–22)

1 *Compare this account with that in Luke 1:26–38. Which parts are similar and which are different?*

The life of Isa

Although Isa was born to a virgin, God was not his father. Muslims say that if God could create Adam without a father, he could also create Isa. The Qur'an tells of Isa's extraordinary powers as a tiny baby because he was able to talk:

'He shall preach to men in his cradle and in the prime of manhood, and shall lead a righteous life.' (3:46)

God also gave Isa miraculous powers as an adult, because the Qur'an says that he could heal the sick of leprosy and blindness and even raise people from the dead. But Isa's most important role was that of a prophet, as he explained:

'I come to confirm the Torah which preceded me and to make lawful to you some of the things you are forbidden. I bring you a sign from your Lord: therefore fear God and obey me. God is my Lord and your Lord: therefore serve Him. That is a straight path.'

When Isa observed that they had no faith, he said: 'Who will help me in the cause of God?'

The disciples replied: 'We are the helpers of God. We believe in God. Bear witness that we have surrendered ourselves to Him.' (3:49–53)

Isa and the Gospel

Muslims believe that God has sent many messages to humanity telling them how they should live. Isa was one of a long line of prophets and he brought people the Injil (Gospel). This was a message from God. It was superseded by the Qur'an, the last message God sent with the prophet Muhammad.

The death of Isa

Muslims do not believe that Isa was crucified, buried or that he came to life on the third day. Instead, they believe he was taken up by God.
The Qur'an says:

'they denied the truth and uttered a monstrous falsehood against Mary. They declared: "We have put to death the Messiah, Jesus the son of Mary, the apostle of God." They did not kill him, nor did they crucify him, but they thought they did... God lifted him up to Himself; God is mighty and wise.' (4:156–158)

2 *Write an entry to go on a Christian website explaining why Muslims hold Jesus in such high regard.*

3 *Draw a Venn diagram to compare the life of Isa with the life of Jesus.*

Son of God

Let's consider the Christian view of Jesus as 'divine'.

The most important Christian belief concerning Jesus is that he was both human and divine (which means that he was part of God) at the same time. This is a difficult idea for anyone to understand because nothing like it exists in our everyday life. To be a Christian, it is essential to accept the concept of Jesus as both man and God as a matter of faith. Christians regularly recite their declaration of faith called the 'Creed'. Let's examine its content.

The Creed

I believe in God, the Father almighty, creator of heaven and earth.

I believe in Jesus Christ, his only Son, our Lord, who was conceived by the Holy Spirit, born of the Virgin Mary, suffered under Pontius Pilate, was crucified, died, and was buried; he descended into the dead.

On the third day he rose again; he ascended into heaven, he is seated at the right hand of the Father, and he will come to judge the living and the dead.

I believe in the Holy Spirit, the Holy Catholic Church, the communion of saints, the forgiveness of sins, the resurrection of the body, and the life everlasting.

Amen

1 *Go through the Creed and list each piece of information which shows that Jesus was the Son of God, rather than an ordinary man.*

People who are not Christian find it difficult to understand why anyone should accept information that goes against normal life. The answer is faith. Maybe this is not as strange as some people might think. There are many things in life that we accept on faith alone and they often concern personal relationships. Will a parent or a lover care for us like they say they will? In the end we have to trust that they will.

This is how the Bible describes God sending his Son to earth.

'The Word became a human being and, full of grace and truth, lived among us. We saw his glory, the glory which he received as the Father's only Son.' (John 1:14)

Gospel stories about Jesus' life relate to three key areas of divine, supernatural intervention:

- The birth stories
- The miracles
- His death and resurrection

2 *Write these three areas on your page. Against each, note down briefly how it was related to Jesus being the Son of God.*

To finish

For Christians, belief in Jesus as the Son of God is arguably the most important one. They believe that by trying to be like him, they will draw closer to God.

Son of Man

Let's examine the reasons why Christians believe that Jesus was human and also why that is so important to Christians.

The Messiah

The Old Testament says several times that God will send a person to solve the world's problems and bring peace. The word 'Messiah' is used to refer to this person. Christians believe that anyone able to solve humanity's problems would need superhuman powers, which could only come from God. But that person would also need to be human in order to live on earth. Christians are sure that Jesus is the Messiah who was promised and therefore he has to be both human and divine, as the following extract says:

The film 'Jesus of Nazareth' set out to show the human side of Jesus.

'The Word became a human being and full of grace and truth, and lived among us. We saw his glory, the glory which he received as the Father's only Son.' (John 1:14)

1 *Put the extract above in your own words, showing which part belongs to the Son of God and which to the Son of Man.*

As a person, Jesus was in the best position to pass God's message directly to people on earth. So it was necessary for Jesus to be born to a human mother and live an ordinary family life with brothers and sisters. One gospel story gives a glimpse of Jesus as a normal young lad, exasperating his mother by wandering off during a family visit to Jerusalem. Luke 2:43–46 says: *'When the festival was over, they started back home, but the boy Jesus stayed in Jerusalem. His parents thought that he was with the group, so they travelled a whole day and then started looking for him among their relatives and friends. They did not find him, so they went back to Jerusalem looking for him...'* Eventually he was found in the Temple learning from the scholars there. You can imagine his parents' reaction!

2 *Draw a diagram to showing how Jesus was the Son of Man.*

Jesus was sent to earth to suffer and die. His sacrifice would pay the price for people's sins and enable people to draw closer to God again.

'The Son of Man will die as God has decided.' (Luke 22:22)

Christians believe that Jesus was prepared to settle the debt people's sins had accrued. To do this, Jesus had to suffer torture and death so that people could be saved and restored to God once more. Gospel stories about the days leading up to Jesus' arrest reveal his human fear at what was to come. His final prayers ask God not to let it happen: *'In great anguish he prayed even more fervently; his sweat was like drops of blood falling to the ground.'* (Luke 22:44)

The accounts of Jesus' torture, death and burial are those of an ordinary man suffering but the stories of Jesus' resurrection three days later are those of the Son of God. No human has ever returned to life after so long.

To finish

3 Write the 'Frequently Asked Questions' section on a Christian website that will help surfers of the Internet to understand how Jesus can be both human and divine. Try to offer reasons to explain why Christians might believe this dual identity was necessary.

Dangerous revolutionary?

Some people think Jesus' teachings were revolutionary. We examine why that was and the effect this has on some Christians today.

MEEK MILD AS IF
Discover the real Jesus

Cute nativity scenes on Christmas cards can lead some people to think that supporting Jesus and his teachings is a nice gentle way of life. That could be true. Jesus, the 'Prince of Peace', has inspired some Christians to become pacifists. However, there is also another way of interpreting Jesus' life and teachings, which is far less comfortable.

Jesus the reformer

One reason that Jesus was arrested and killed was because he challenged the rules. The Romans mistakenly thought he was going to start a military rebellion to overthrow them and the Jews thought he was threatening the future of their religion.

He upset other people by encouraging women to take a more active part in society than before, allowing them to sit with men and learn. This was at a time when a woman's place was firmly in the home. Stories also show he would help anyone who needed it, such as people with diseases who were outcasts from society. He also helped people who were non-Jewish, like himself. What upset the Jewish authorities most was that Jesus healed people on the Sabbath day – a day when work was forbidden. What Jesus' actions were saying was that compassion is more important than 'the rules'. Something the authorities totally disagreed with.

Jesus the pacifist

Jesus' teachings were revolutionary in another way. He emphasised the need for peaceful, non-violent solutions, which some took as a sign of weakness. Jesus told his followers:

'Do not take revenge on someone who wrongs you. If anyone slaps you on the right cheek let him slap your left cheek too.' (Matthew 10:34–39)

This is not the action of a coward or weakling. Experience may have taught you that one way of defeating bullies can be to stand up to them.

Take action!

There were other times when Jesus indicated that a completely different reaction was necessary. He told his followers:

'Do not think that I have come to bring peace to the world. No, I did not come to bring peace, but a sword.' (Matthew 10:34)

When he sent his disciples out on a mission on one occasion, they were told:

'Whoever has a purse or a bag must take it; and whoever has no sword must sell his coat and buy one.' (Luke 22:36)

Liberation theology

The fact that Jesus was prepared to challenge society and not ignore the injustices of his day has inspired some modern Christians. They argue that if Jesus was alive on earth today, he wouldn't just sit in church praying. He'd try to do something about world poverty and human rights abuse. These Christians argue that violent action may sometimes be necessary to defeat evil. Only when evil is defeated will peace have a chance.

A movement began in South America that involved priests and believers doing something to help the poor and oppressed, even if that action involved breaking the law. Some priests have left their comfortable housing and gone to live and work alongside the poor. More controversially, others have become involved in violent action aimed at bringing about political change.

Not surprisingly, this 'Liberation theology', as it is called, is not approved of by the Church. In fact, Pope John Paul II told Catholics that taking part in revolutionary struggles is not how Christians should go about helping the poor.

1. *Why do you think some Christians say that taking direct political action is not the right way to sort out social problems? What's your opinion?*
2. *What sort of ways of tackling poverty do you think Pope John Paul II would have preferred? Which do you think works and why?*
3. *Reply to the following letter:*

'I've always been a Christian and I don't think it's right for priests to live in slums. What good can this do?'

Picture this!

Look at these three different images of Jesus and decide what the artists were trying to say about his personality through each picture.

WAY OUT
SLOANE ST
KNIGHTSBRIDGE

6.7

6.8 Just to recap

6.9

In this unit of work we have been considering the different aspects of Jesus which have made him one of the most important people to have lived. We have considered what is known about him and the inspiration he has given to Christians.

Let's remind ourselves of what we have learned:

We began by examining the interest that Jesus' life generates today. **A** What example can you give of interest in Jesus' life today? **B** Why might some people rank him as one of the top ten men in history?	**We went on to look** at the historical Jesus and the Muslim Jesus. **A** What is the Arabic name for Jesus? **B** Give three pieces of historical evidence that point to the existence of Jesus as a historical character.
We studied in detail Jesus as both a human being and the Son of God. **A** Why do Christians believe Jesus was the Son of God? **B** Why was it necessary for Jesus to be human?	**We examined** the idea of Jesus as a revolutionary figure. **A** Give two things Jesus did that were thought of as revolutionary. **B** What is 'Liberation theology'?

We started out with the idea that many people think Jesus was someone special. At the end of the study, have you understood some of the reasons that lead Christians to think this?

This is the side of Lake Galilee where Jesus carried out many of his teachings. How important do you think it is for there to be historical evidence to support belief?

Choose one of the following tasks to check your progress in this unit.

Task one

a *Give two things that the Qur'an says about Isa that show this is the same person as Jesus.*

b *Explain the difference between the idea of Jesus as the Son of Man and the Son of God.*

c *'Jesus lived and died 2000 years ago. It's all over now.' Why do you think some people believe that? What would a Christian say to that statement? Would you say it's true or not?*

Task two

a *Why do some Christians describe Jesus as a revolutionary?*

b *Explain what sort of things can be proved about Jesus and what sort of things can't.*

c *'It doesn't really matter if some of the stories about Jesus have become exaggerated because what he stood for can only do good.' What do you think about this statement? What sort of reasons would people who disagreed with you give?*

6.9 Something extra

1 *Why do Christians believe that it was necessary for Jesus to have a virgin mother?*

2 *Pictured right is the Baptist minister, Martin Luther King. He was inspired by Jesus to fight against the oppression that black people were suffering in America. His battle against injustice was a non-violent one. Use the Internet to research some information about his campaign, especially the bus boycott that took place in December 1955. When you have gathered enough information, design a poster that Martin Luther King could have used to tell people how to protest and why it should not be violent.*

3 *'Do not take revenge on someone who wrongs you. If anyone slaps you on the right cheek, let him slap your left cheek too.' (Matthew 10:34–39) What is revolutionary about this sort of advice from Jesus? How could it work?*

4 *Create a mind map showing some of the different facets of Jesus' personality.*

5

Memo: Forward Planning

Subject: We are interested in getting one of Jesus' followers on next Thursday's chat show. Who do you suggest?

Message: Topics that might interest the viewers include:
How revolutionary was he?
What sort of claims did people make for him?
What attracted the crowds?

Can you supply Adrian with some notes for guidance on these points?

Any other good areas to explore?

6 *Shown above are the statues of some people from the twentieth century who were inspired to stand up for what they believed in because Jesus did.*

Choose two of the following people to research further and produce a folded A4 leaflet about their lives and deaths: St Elizabeth of Russia, Manche Masemola, Esther John, Maximilian Kolbe, Lucian Tapiedi, Dietrich Bonhoeffer, Wang Zhiming, Janani Luwum, Oscar Romero and Martin Luther King.

7 *Complete an acrostic poem based on the word JESUS. Try to include some of the different aspects of Jesus.*

J

E

S

U

S

Glossary

9/11 The name given to the terrorist attack on the Twin Towers of the World Trade Center in New York in 2001: 3000 people were killed.

A

Abortion The deliberate removal of a foetus from the womb so that it dies.

Acrostic A poem that takes each letter in a word and uses it to begin the next line.

Act of God A term which insurance companies use for natural disasters that are not covered in their policies. This may include events such as earthquakes and lightning strikes.

Acupuncture An alternative medical treatment that uses fine needles to help the body heal itself.

Adam and Eve Traditionally the first people on earth, according to the book of Genesis in the Bible.

Agnostic A person who is not sure whether God exists or not.

Allah The Arabic term for God that is used by Muslims.

Atheist A person who is convinced God does not exist.

Auschwitz A concentration camp in World War II, where thousands of Jews were murdered.

B

Big Bang Theory A scientific theory which states that the universe was formed as a result of a cosmic explosion. This is widely accepted.

Blog An internet diary that is available for anyone to read.

C

Conjoined twins Twins that are born joined to each other as a result of a malformation in the womb. They used to be called 'Siamese twins'.

Creationist A Christian who believes that the universe was formed in six days, in exactly the way it is described in the book of Genesis.

Creed A Christian declaration of belief that is recited regularly in Church services.

D

David Hume A Scottish eighteenth-century philosopher.

Design argument The argument that says God must exist because the world could not have happened by accident.

Designer babies A modern medical procedure which would enable a couple to choose the sort of baby they will have in terms of sex, hair colour and so on. This is very controversial because it involves destroying foetuses that do not match the couple's requirements.

DNA A scientific code which all living beings have. It has been called the pattern of life. Each being's code is unique.

Donor organs Body parts that are voluntarily given to someone else who has a faulty organ. This might involve a heart or cornea (part of the eye) given after death, or one kidney donated while the person is still alive.

E

Embryo The early stages of human or animal life in the womb. It could be called a foetus.

Euthanasia Agreeing to assist a person to die in order to save him or her further suffering.

F

Foetus The early stages of human or animal life in the womb. It could be called an embryo.

Free will The freedom to choose what you will do, that is not dictated by another person or higher power.

G

Ganesh The Hindu god with the body of a person and the head of an elephant.

Garden of Eden The traditional place where, according to the Bible, Adam and Eve lived. It was a place of perfection.

Genetically modified These are cells which have been altered to include genetic material from another organism. They are sometimes called GM.

Genetic engineering Modern scientific techniques that involve removing genetic material from one organism and replacing it with material from another. This might be between the same species but could involve placing animal DNA in a plant.

H

Haiku A Japanese poem in three lines of five, seven and five syllables.

Hospice A place where people who are terminally ill can be cared for.

Human Genome Project The mapping of the full set of human chromosomes.

Humanists A group of people who do not believe in God or any religion, but have a moral code based on respecting people as fellow human beings.

I

Isa The Arabic name for Jesus, used by Muslims.

IVF treatment A method of human reproduction that involves fertilization of a female egg with sperm outside the body, then placing the embryo back in the woman's body.

J

Jibril The Arabic name for the angel Gabriel in Islam.

K

Karma The religious belief that everything we do has an effect. The consequences of a person's behaviour may be felt in this life or in a future one.

L

Lakshmi A popular Hindu goddess of good fortune, who is often shown with gold coins showering from her hand.

Liberation theology A belief held by some Christians that it is acceptable to break the law or to use violence in order to bring about the Kingdom of God.

Lourdes A well-known pilgrimage site for Roman Catholics in the south of France, where St Bernadette had a vision of the Virgin Mary.

M

Messiah The belief that God will send someone to solve the problems of the world. Christians believe this person was Jesus.

Miracle A good event that cannot be explained.

Mother Theresa A Roman Catholic nun who founded a charity to care for the sick and dying in India. She died in 1997 and is being made a saint.

N

Natural selection A widely-held scientific theory that plant and animal life has evolved so that only the fittest survive.

O

Ouija Board A supernatural activity in which people try to receive messages from the dead spelled out from an alphabet on the table.

P

Padre Pio A Roman Catholic priest in Italy who died in 1968; he displayed signs of the stigmata on his head, hands and feet. In 2002 he was made a saint.

Paley William Paley was an eighteenth-century Christian philosopher who used the Design argument to prove the existence of God.

Pilgrimage A special journey to a holy place for religious reasons.

Placebo effect When a patient recovers from an illness after taking tablets they believed to be prescription drugs. In reality the tablets contained no drugs and it was the person's trust in medicine that healed them.

Prince of Peace A title Christians give Jesus showing they believe he came to bring love and peace to the world.

Q

Quakers A group of Christians who think that what you do is more important than what you believe. They have no set prayers, leaders or ceremonies in their worship.

R

Ramadan The holy month in the Islamic calendar when Muslims fast during the hours of daylight.

Resurrection of Jesus The time when Jesus came to life again after he had been dead for three days.

Roman Catholic The largest Christian denomination in the world. It is led by the Pope.

S

Sanctity of Life The belief that human life is special and sacred.

Satan Another name for the devil.

Shiva One of the major Hindu gods who is responsible for life and death, creation and destruction.

Son of God A title given to Jesus showing he is divine because God was his father.

Son of Man A title Christians give Jesus showing that he is both divine and human because he was born to an earthly mother.

Stigmata Open wounds that are said to appear on the hands, feet, head and side of a holy person in order that they can share in the suffering of Jesus. This phenomenon is unique to Roman Catholic Christians.

Supernatural experience Something that cannot be explained by any known scientific theories.

Supreme Spirit The name Hindus use for God.

T

Theory of Evolution An explanation of the way humans evolved from apes. This explanation, first worked out by Charles Darwin, is now widely accepted.

The Temple During the time of Jesus, this was the most important Jewish place of worship. It was in Jerusalem.

Tsunami A destructive tidal wave caused by an earthquake in the ocean. The most severe one in modern times occurred on Boxing Day 2004.

V

Vivisection Experiments performed on animals without the use of anaesthetics.

Index